"Marketing Management"

Dr. Brijesh Sivathamu

FIRST EDITION

LAXMI BOOK PUBLICATION
258/34, Raviwar Peth,
Solapur-413005
Cell: +91 9595359435

Rs: 150 /-

"Marketing Management"

Dr. Brijesh Sivathamu

© 2014 by Laxmi Book Publication, Solapur

ISBN :

Published by,
Laxmi Book Publication,
258/34, Raviwar Peth,
Solapur, Maharashtra, India

Contact No. : +91 9595 359 435
Website : http://www.isrj.net
Email ID : ayisrj@yahoo.in

INDEX

Chapter 1

PREFACE

It is indeed a matter of great pleasure for me to present this book to our esteemed readers. This book has been designed as a standard book on Marketing Management for the M.B.A. course.

This book comprehensively covers the entire syllabus of the MBA course of University of Pune effective from June 2013 onwards. While writing this book, special care has been taken to meet the requirements of the students of MBA.

Some of the special features of this book are as follows:

1. Full coverage of the revised syllabus of MBA.
2. Point-wise explanation of each topic in every chapter.
3. Extensive use of graphics, tables and various forms to give visual view of the key concepts and techniques.
4. Topics are logically arranged in paragraphs exactly according to the revised syllabus.
5. Practical implications of Marketing Management have been demonstrated with the help of case studies, real life examples and illustrations.

Every effort has been made to provide the readers with the most up to date and authentic material on the subject.

I am very grateful to the publisher Mr. Ashok Yakkaldevi of M/s Laxmi Publication who has rendered all possible assistance in bringing out this book.

I will consider my efforts to be amply rewarded in case this book proves to be useful to the students and teachers of the subject.

Suggestions and feedback of the readers are welcome and shall be acknowledged with gratitude for improvements in future editions.

With best wishes,

Dr. Brijesh Sivathanu

ACKNOWLEDGEMENTS

Getting a finished book into the hands of a reader requires the work and efforts of many people. The author does his part by efficiently developing an outline, thoroughly researching the topics, writing about these topics and developing the learning activities.

I would like to recognize all the people who contributed directly or indirectly to this text book. I wish to acknowledge my sincere gratitude to all those who assisted and helped me in preparing this book. First are the reviewers, as the author cannot survive without the good feedback from the reviewers and I sincerely appreciate their suggestions that were given to me. I would also like to thank the top management of my institute who provided me the motivation, guidance and valuable suggestions without which this would not be possible.

A book doesn't simply appear automatically on the bookstore shelves. It can only get there with the combined and sincere efforts of the entire publishing team at M/s Lama Publications.

My special thanks are due to my parents and family members for their extensive support and constant motivation.

Dr. Brines Sivathanu

UNIT 1: NEW PRODUCT DEVELOPMENT & PRODUCT LIFE CYCLE

MODULE 1.1 NEW PRODUCT DEVELOPMENT

Product

Products are an important variable in the marketing mix. The mix of products offered by a company such as Heinz can be a firm's most important competitive tool. If a company's products do not meet customers 'desires and needs, the company will fail unless it makes adjustments. Developing successful products like Dell personal computers requires knowledge of fundamental product concepts.

A product is a good, a service, or an idea received in an exchange.

- It can be either tangible or intangible and includes functional, social, and psychological utilities or benefits.
- It also includes supporting services, such as installation, guarantees, product information, and promises of repair or maintenance.
- Thus the four-year/50,000-km warranty that covers some new automobiles is part of the product itself.

A good is a tangible physical entity, such as a Dell personal computer or a McAloo Tikki.

A service, in contrast, is intangible; it is the result of the application of human and mechanical efforts to people or objects. Examples of services include a performance by Jagjit Singh, online travel agencies, medical examinations, child day care, real estate services, and martial arts lessons.

An idea is a concept, philosophy, image, or issue. Ideas provide the psychological stimulation that aids in solving problems or adjusting to the environment. For example, India Against Corruption campaign by Team Anna in 2012 or Run for Unity campaign by Narendra Modi led BJP in 2013 to pay tribute to Sardar Vallahbhai Patel.

Figure 1: The total Product

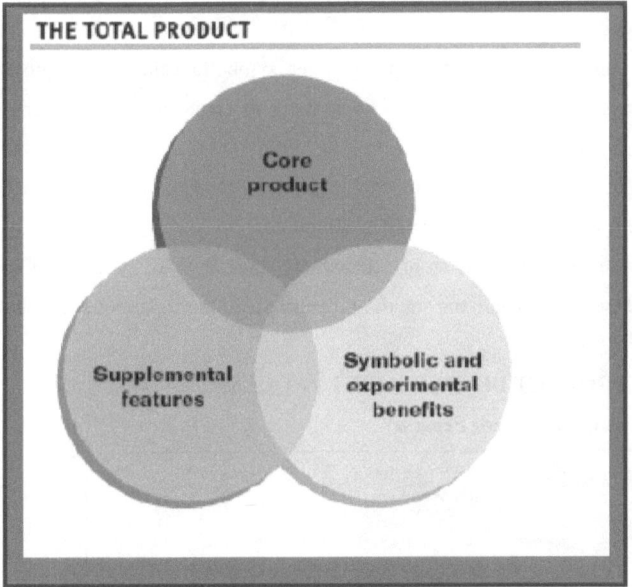

It is helpful to think of a total product offering as having three interdependent elements: the core product itself, its supplemental features, and its symbolic or experiential benefits. Consider that some people buy new tires for their basic utility (e.g., CEAT, Apollo), whereas some look for safety (e.g., Michelin, Bridgestone), and others buy on the basis of brand name or exemplary performance (e.g., Pirelli).

- **The core product** consists of a product's fundamental utility or main benefit and usually addresses a fundamental need of the consumer. Broadband Internet services, for instance, offer speedy Internet access, but some buyers want additional features, such as wireless connectivity anywhere they go.
- **Supplemental features** provide added value or attributes in addition to the core utility or benefit. Supplemental products also can provide installation, delivery, training, and financing. These supplemental attributes are not required to make the core product function effectively, but they help to differentiate one product brand from another.

- **Symbolic and Experimental Benefits.** Finally, customers also receive benefits based on their experiences with the product. In addition, many products have symbolic meaning for buyers.

For some consumers, the simple act of shopping gives symbolic value and improves their attitudes. Some stores capitalize on this value by striving to create a special experience for customers.\

For example, you can buy stuffed toys at many retailers, but at Foto Fast you can choose the type of animal, personalize it with your dear ones name, and photo.

The atmosphere and decor of a retail store, the variety and depth of product choices, the customer support, and even the sounds and smells all contribute to the experiential element.

MODULE 1.2 NEW PRODUCT DEVELOPMENT PROCESS

Figure 2: New Product Development Process

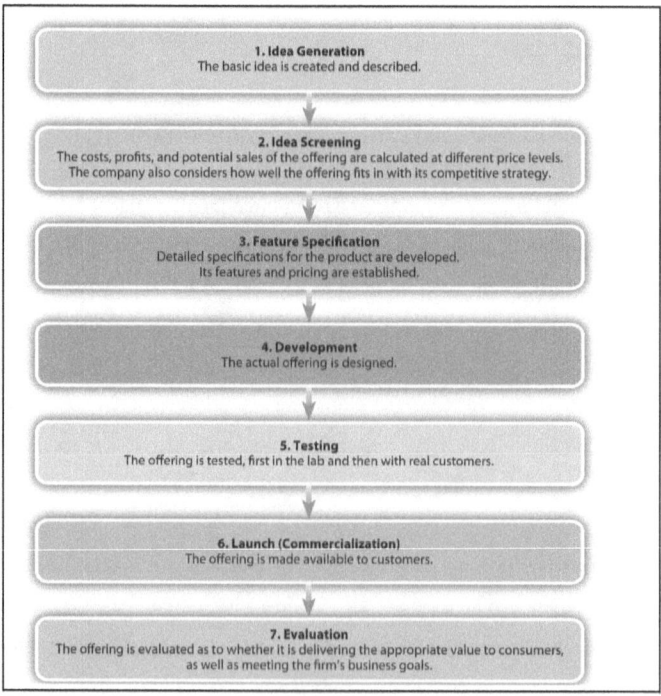

1. Idea Generation

New product development starts with idea generation – the systematic search for new product ideas. A company typically generates hundreds of ideas, even thousands, in order to find a few good ones.

Good ideas are the life blood of new product development. This raises the question: _What constitutes a —good idea?'

Evidence on the mortality rates involved in developing new products means that we need a lot of ideas before we are likely to find one that constitutes a winner. Two key aspects are involved in increasing the number of ideas for new products, namely:

1. an effective scanning process for new ideas which systematically collects ideas for possible new products from the widest range of sources possible;
2. the use of the techniques of _creativity' to encourage idea generation.
3. There are two sources for idea generation – Internal Sources and External Sources

a. Internal Sources

- New-product ideas can come from several sources. They may come from internal sources—marketing managers, researchers, sales personnel, engineers, or other organizational personnel. Brainstorming and incentives or rewards for good ideas are typical intra-firm devices for stimulating development of ideas.
- For example, the idea for 3M Post-it Notes came from an employee. As a church choir member, he used slips of paper to mark songs in his hymnal. Because the pieces of paper fell out, he suggested developing an adhesive-backed note. In the restaurant industry, ideas may come from franchisees.
- At McDonald's, for example, franchise owners invented the Big Mac and the Egg McMuff in. Today, new McDonald's product ideas often come from corporate chef Dan Coudreaut, who developed the fast-food giant's new snack wrap.

Case-let: IBM's Innovation Jam

In July 2006, IBM kicked off a defining moment in collaborative innovation: arguably the largest online brainstorming session ever held. The event was the IBM ® Innovation Jam ® and it attracted more than 150,000 participants from 104 countries and 67 different companies over the course of two 72-hour sessions.

They were drawn by IBM CEO Sam Palmisano's objective to invest up to US$100 million to develop and bring to market the best ideas from the event. Their dialog resulted in tens of thousands of creative and far-reaching ideas, many of which are already having an impact on business and society today.

We opened up our labs, said to the world, _Here are our crown jewels, have at them,' said Palmisano. He had good reason to share: an earlier visit to the company's labs had convinced him that many great ideas were percolating, but behind closed doors. In his mind, they weren't going to escape into the market using traditional development methods.

It was an earlier jam—Values Jam, in 2003—that crystallized the core IBM value of —Innovation that matters.

—But there were still gaps in our capabilities, still people who confused technological invention with true innovation, said David Yaun, a corporate communications vice president who ran IBM's innovation programs at the time.

—Experiential programs like Innovation Jam featured both the outcomes and the collaborative nature of true innovation

In that regard, IBM's jams represent a new form of organizational intervention, a way to accelerate change. As their name suggests, these jams are like jazz improvisations, connecting people who might otherwise never meet, allowing them to formulate and build on each other's thoughts, and in the process, create something entirely new. Because they are radically open and democratic

— everybody has the same capacity to participate, regardless of level or expertise—jams speak to the expectations of today's professional worker.

While Innovation Jam was novel because it included external participants, jamming was already a way of life for IBMers. The process grew out of the company's rapid embrace of its intranet in the late 1990s. Research showed that IBMers trusted and relied on their intranet at unprecedented Levels even more than their managers or the grapevine. Seeking to develop and extend that trust, the company introduced World Jam in 2001. This event drew upon experiences in online collaboration, including IBM's own VM Fora in the 1980s, as well as in-person jams held in

IBM Research labs in the late 1990s. In the process, IBMers invented a new medium, something beyond online communities, brainstorming sessions, or traditional suggestion systems.

As IBM's chairman Sam Palmisano put it in an interview with *Harvard Business Review*, —You just can't impose command-and-control mechanisms on a large, highly professional workforce. Palmisano sees unfiltered dialog not as a drawback but as a tremendous benefit for a leader: —Youcould say, 'Oh my God, I've unleashed this incredible negative energy.' Or you could say, _Oh my God, I now have this incredible mandate to drive even more change in the company.'

Jamming also speeds implementation of the new ideas and plans it brings to the surface—in part because they are already pre-socialized. Following an initial 72-hour Innovation Jam session that resulted in 46,000 posts, the most promising suggestions were distilled, and 31 ideas were brought forward for further refinement and validation in the next phase of the jam.

In the second phase, jammers grappled with a new set of questions: What competition for a given idea is out there? Would you be willing to use the idea yourself? How can our clients and IBMgenerate profit from it? Wikis were set around each big idea to help collaboratively build basic business plans and use scenarios. Some ideas held up to the scrutiny and got stronger, while others fell by the wayside.

Ten promising ideas surfaced and entered an accelerated development program sponsored by IBM executive vice president Nick Donofrio. The most successful of these projects—including the creation of an on-demand system for real-time analysis of traffic flow; infusing intelligence into the world's utility grids; the introduction of smart healthcare payment systems and a new business unit to provide solutions and services that would directly benefit the environment—became part of the IBM Smarter Planet agenda, and have since generated billions of US dollars in revenue for the company.

Today, jams have become part of IBM's management system and culture; a second Innovation Jam took place in 2008. They have also spawned a consulting service offered to the company's clients.

Jams are used for many purposes: from organizational transformation, to best-practice capture, to societal change on a global scale. One example is Habitat Jam in 2005, collaboration among

IBM, the United Nations and the government of Canada to shape the agenda of the UN-HABITAT organization's biennial World Urban Forum.

In the end, jamming is a new medium for an old purpose. It continues IBM's century-long history of innovating the process of innovation itself—from classic research, to open source and social media,15to the cross-societal collaborations of the company's Smarter Planet agenda. In particular, World Jam and its progeny have helped move IBM from the Web 1.0 era—with its focus on content and publishing—into the era of Web 2.0 and beyond, to what some are calling —social business, where IBM is continuing to be a pioneer. In that history of collaborative innovation, IBM's jams hold an important place—and they continue to play an important role today.

b. External Sources

- New-product ideas also may arise from sources outside the firm, such as customers, competitors, advertising agencies, management consultants, and research organizations.
- Procter & Gamble gets 35 percent of its ideas from inventors and outside consultants. Consultants are often used as sources for stimulating new product ideas.
- Home Depot got the idea for its new Orange Works architect-designed fire extinguisher from Arnell Group, a marketing and design company; Arnell Group's founder once worked for architect Michael Graves, who provided ideas and designs for many new products at retail giant Target.

2. Screening

- In the process of **screening,** the ideas with the greatest potential are selected for further review. During screening, product ideas are analyzed to determine whether or not they match the organization's objectives and resources.
- If a product idea results in a product similar to the firm's existing products, marketers must assess the degree to which the new product could cannibalize the sales of current products. The company's overall abilities to produce and market the product are also analyzed.

- Other aspects of an idea to be weighed are the nature and wants of buyers and possible environmental changes. Compared with other phases, the greatest number of new-product ideas is rejected during the screening phase.

3. Concept Testing

- To evaluate ideas properly, it may be necessary to test product concepts. In **concept testing,** a small sample of potential buyers is presented with a product idea through written or oral description (and perhaps a few drawings) to determine their attitudes and initial buying intentions regarding the product.
- For a single product idea, an organization can test one or several concepts of the same product. Concept testing is a low-cost procedure that allows a company to determine customers'initial reactions to a product idea before it invests considerable resources in research and development. Input from online communities also may be beneficial in the product development process.
- The results of concept testing can help product development personnel better understand which product attributes and benefits are most important to potential customers.

4. Marketing Strategy Development

If the results of the concept testing stage are encouraging, the next step in the new product development process is the formulation of preliminary marketing strategy plans for the product launch which include:
- preliminary marketing objectives;
- delineation of possible market targets;
- product positioning strategies;
- preliminary marketing mix decisions;
- Preliminary budget estimates.

5. Business Analysis

- During the **business analysis** stage, the product idea is evaluated to determine its potential contribution to the firm's sales, costs, and profits. In the business analysis stage, firms seek market information.
- The results of consumer polls, along with secondary data, supply the specifics needed to estimate potential sales, costs, and profits. For many products in this stage (when they are still just product ideas), forecasting sales accurately is difficult.
- This is especially true for innovative and completely new products. Organizations sometimes employ breakeven analysis to determine how many units they would have to sell to begin making a profit. At times, an organization also uses payback analysis, in which marketers compute the time period required to recover the funds that would be invested in developing the new product.
- Because breakeven and payback analyses are based on estimates, they are usually viewed as useful but not particularly precise tools.

6. Product development

- Product development is the phase in which the organization determines if it is technically feasible to produce the product and if it can be produced at costs low enough to make the final price reasonable.
- If business analysis points to a favorable decision, the next major step is product development which is where costs tend to rise substantially. □ Once a physical product e.g. a prototype, has been developed, further testing, both technical and consumer, should be carried out. Even at this stage an objective and critical view needs to be taken about further investment in the product.

7. Test marketing

- This is the penultimate stage before full scale commercialization and launch. Here, the new product is tested in a way that involves consumers purchasing in a normal shopping situation, or in the case of a more durable product, being tested in an environment in which it is finally used (usually in the home).

- This process is conducted towards the end of the development process when the concept, product and marketing strategy are at a refined stage.
- The objective of the test marketing exercise is reduction of risk in any subsequent decisions that are made. The need for this research is to reduce the risk of a costly mistake in a national launch.

Types of Test Marketing

Simulated store test –

- This method uses a small sample of consumers (usually 30-40) to test their initial response to a product. The consumers will be shown advertising for a range of products including your own (if this is applicable) and those from competitors.
- They then _shop'in a simulated store fixture, while being observed throughout, and later interviewed about what choices they have made. While this is a fairly artificial test, it does provide useful information in a controlled way and at an early stage.
- Advantages of this method are that the results are quick and advertising effectiveness cane evaluated. The cost of implementing this method is less than that of standard or controlled test markets.
- Advances in research and technology have provided improvements to this type of test in Recent years.
- However, this method is arguably more rooted in research than reality and, therefore, may be considered less of a test market.

Controlled test –
- This is where a number of locations or trade customers will be used as the test area. The product is launched into the test area and elements like product, promotion, placement and price can be controlled.
- However, it is not possible to replicate full plans like advertising or media promotions. This method is generally quicker and less expensive than standard test marketing. However, the trade-off is that it can be less representative, so more caution may have tube exercised when reading the results.

- This method also uses a smaller sample base than standard testing.

Standard test marketing –

- This method most accurately replicates a full-scale national launch. Geographic areas are chosen (it could be towns, cities or a region of the country).
- The results will often be monitored versus the control area (e.g. the rest of the country), to give a full understanding of the change in consumer behavior your product launch has affected.
- This method of testing is really a trial run for the major launch and all elements of the sales and marketing plan should be assessed e.g. from reaction at store level and stock turn around to levels of trial and repeat purchase.
- While this is the most effective of testing methods, it is also the most expensive and time consuming.

8. Commercialization

- The final stage of new product development is _commercialization‘, or bringing the product to the market. If the company goes ahead with commercialization, it is likely to begin to incur its highest costs, involving as it does investment in plant and production and marketing costs.
- As a consequence care and planning is required if the product is to succeed: many otherwise excellent products have failed because of an inadequately managed launch phase.

MODULE 1.3 BRANDING

BRANDING

A brand is a name, term, design, symbol, or any other feature that identifies one marketer's product as distinct from those of other marketers.

- A brand may identify a single item, a family of items, or all items of that seller. Some have defined a brand as not just the physical good, name, color, logo, or ad campaign but everything associated with the product, including its symbolism and experiences.

- A **brand name** is the part of a brand that can be spoken—including letters, words, and numbers—such as 7Up.
- A brand name is often a product's only distinguishing characteristic. Without the brand name, a firm could not differentiate its products. To consumers, a brand name is as fundamental as the product itself.
- The element of a brand that is not made up of words—often a symbol or design—is **brand mark.** Examples of brand marks include McDonald's Golden Arches, Nike's—swoosh, and the stylized silhouette of Apple's iPod.
- **Trademark** is a legal designation indicating that the owner has exclusive use of a brander a part of a brand and that others are prohibited by law from using it.
- Finally, a **trade name** is the full and legal name of an organization, such as Ford Motor Company, rather than the name of a specific product.
- **Value of Branding** Both buyers and sellers benefit from branding. Brands help **buyers** to identify specific products that they do and do not like which, intern, facilitates the purchase of items that satisfy their needs and reduces the time required to purchase the product.
- Without brands, product selection would be quite random because buyers could have no assurance that they were purchasing what they preferred. The purchase of certain brands can be a form of self-expression.
- For example, clothing brand names are important to many consumers. Names such as Tommy Hilfiger, Polo, Nike, and Guess give manufacturers an advantage in the marketplace.
- Especially when a customer is unable to judge a product's quality, a brand may symbolize a certain quality level to the customer, and in turn, the person lets that perception of quality represent the quality of the item.
- A brand helps to reduce a buyer's perceived risk of purchase. In addition, a psychological reward may come from owning a brand that symbolizes status. The Mercedes-Benz brandies an example. **Sellers benefit** from branding because each company's brands identify its products, which makes repeat purchasing easier for customers.
- Branding helps a firm to introduce a new product that carries the name of one or more of its existing products because buyers are already familiar with the firm's existing brands.

- It facilitates promotional efforts because the promotion of each branded product indirectly promotes all other similarly branded products.
- Branding also fosters brand loyalty. To the extent that buyers become loyal to a specific brand, the company's market share for that product achieves a certain level of stability, allowing the firm to use its resources more efficiently.

Once a firm develops some degree of customer loyalty for a brand, it can maintain a fairly consistent price rather than continually cutting the price to attract customers.

BRAND EQUITY

A well-managed brand is an asset to an organization. The value of this asset is often referred to as brand equity.

Brand equity is the marketing and financial value associated with a brand's strength in a market. Besides the actual proprietary brand assets, such as patents and trademarks, four major elements underlie brand equity: brand name awareness, brand loyalty, perceived brand quality, and brand associations

Building Brand Equity

Marketers build brand equity by creating the right brand knowledge structures with the right consumers. This process depends on *all* brand-related contacts—whether marketer-initiated or not. From a marketing management perspective, however, there are three main sets of *brand equity drivers:*

1. *The initial choices for the brand elements or identities making up the brand (brand names, URLs, logos, symbols, characters, spokespeople, slogans, jingles, packages, and signage)—*
   Microsoft chose the name Bing for its new search engine because it felt it unambiguously conveyed search and the —aha‖ moment of finding what a person is looking for. It is also short, appealing, memorable, active, and effective multicultural.

2. *The product and service and all accompanying marketing activities and supporting marketing programs*—Liz Claiborne's fastest-growing label is Juicy Couture, whose edgy, contemporary sportswear and accessories have a strong lifestyle appeal to women, men, and kids. Positioned as an affordable luxury, the brand creates its exclusive cachet via limited distribution and a somewhat risqué name and rebellious attitude.

3. *Other associations indirectly transferred to the brand by linking it to some other entity (adperson, place, or thing)*—The brand name of New Zealand vodka 42BELOW refers to both latitude that runs through New Zealand and the percentage of its alcohol content. The packaging and other visual cues are designed to leverage the perceived purity of the country to communicate the positioning for the brand.

Choosing Brand Elements

Brand elements are devices, which can be trademarked, that identify and differentiate the brand. Most strong brands employ multiple brand elements. Nike has the distinctive —swoosh‖ logo, the empowering —Just Do It‖ slogan, and the —Nike‖ name from the Greek winged goddess of victory.

Marketers should choose brand elements to build as much brand equity as possible. The test is what consumers would think or feel about the product *if* the brand element were all they knew. Based on its name alone, for instance, a consumer might expect Snack Well's products to be healthful snack foods and Panasonic Tough book laptop computers to be durable and reliable.

BRAND ELEMENT CHOICE CRITERIA There are six criteria for choosing brand elements. The first three—memorable, meaningful, and likable—are —brand building. The latter three—transferable, adaptable, and protectable—are —defensive‖ and help leverage and preserve brand equity against challenges.

1. *Memorable*—How easily do consumers recall and recognize the brand element, and when—at both purchase and consumption? Short names such as Tide, Crest, and Puffs are memorable brand elements.

2. *Meaningful*—Is the brand element credible? Does it suggest the corresponding category and a product ingredient or the type of person who might use the brand? Consider the inherent meaning in names such as Duracell auto batteries.
3. *Likable*—How aesthetically appealing is the brand element? A recent trend is for playful names that also offer a readily available URL, like Flicker photo sharing, Face book social networking, and Motorola's ROKR and RAZR cell phones.
4. *Transferable*—Can the brand element introduce new products in the same or different categories? Does it add to brand equity across geographic boundaries and market segments?

Although initially an online book seller, Amazon.com was smart enough not to call itself —Books R'Us The Amazon is famous as the world's biggest river, and the name suggests the wide variety of goods that could be shipped, an important descriptor of the diverse range of products the company now sells.

5. *Adaptable*—How adaptable and updatable is the brand element? The face of Betty Crocker has received more than seven makeovers in 87 years, and she doesn't look a day over 35!
6. *Protectable*—How legally protectable is the brand element? How competitively protectable? Names that become synonymous with product categories—such as Dada, Scotch Tape, Xerox, and Fiberglass—should retain their trademark rights and not become generic.

Types of Brands

There are three categories of brands: manufacturer, private distributor, and generic.

- **Manufacturer brands** are initiated by producers and ensure that producers are identified with their products at the point of purchase—for example, Green Giant, Dell, Starbucks, and Levi's jeans. A manufacturer brand usually requires a producer to become involved in distribution, promotion, and to some extent, pricing decisions.
- **Private distributor brands** (also called *private brands, store brands,* or *dealer brands*) are initiated and owned by resellers—wholesalers or retailers. The major characteristic of

private brands is that the manufacturers are not identified on the products. Retailers and wholesalers use private distributor brands to develop more efficient promotion, generate higher gross margins, and change store image.

- Some marketers of traditionally branded products have embarked on a policy of not branding, often called *generic branding*. **Generic brands** indicate only the product category (such as aluminum foil) and do not include the company name or other identifying terms. Generic brands usually are sold at lower prices than comparable branded items.

MODULE 1.4 PACKAGING AND LABELING

- **Packaging** includes all the activities of designing and producing the container for product.
- Packages might have up to three layers. Davidoff cologne comes in a bottle (*primary package*) in a cardboard box (*secondary package*) in a corrugated box (*shipping package*) containing six dozen bottles in cardboard boxes.
- The package is the buyer's first encounter with the product. A good package draws the consumer in and encourages product choice. In effect, they can act as —five-second commercials‖ for the product.
- Packaging also affects consumers'later product experiences when they go to open the package and use the product at home. Some packages can even be attractively displayed at home. Distinctive packaging like that for Kiwi shoe polish and Absolute vodka is an important part of a brand's equity.

Packaging must achieve a number of objectives:

1. Identify the brand.
2. Convey descriptive and persuasive information.
3. Facilitate product transportation and protection.
4. Assist at-home storage.
5. Aid product consumption.

Lifebuoy to get a facelift – Economic Times

Rajas Kalka, TEN Feb 9, 2002,

Mumbai: Hindustan lever, the country's largest consumer goods company, and will prelaunch its 107-year old lifebuoy brand in an attempt to upgrade its image and positioning. This will be the first major prelaunch of the soap and it will transform lifebuoy from a low-end, mass product into a brand new soap with a new price, packaging and positioning. Sources said the company is reducing the size of the normal lifebuoy soap to 125 gms from 150 gms and increasing the price to Rs 9 from Rs 8.50, an effective hike of 27 per cent. The company will make a formal announcement on February 12. Company officials remained tightlipped about the issue. When contacted, an HLL spokesman declined to comment. Analysts say lever is attempting to revive the brand's fortunes which have declined recently due to falling volumes in the overall soap segment. Lifebuoy commands a volume market share of 18 per cent and is one of the most successful brands in the lever stable. But it has recently lost market share in a declining soaps market and its value dipped to Rs 450 core in 2001 from Rs 595 crore in 2000. The price hike will come close on the heels of similar moves by lever in other products in the personal wash category. They believe that the current stock price of HLL has already taken into account the price revision to be announced by HLL. "The current price factors in the increase in prices of key brands like Lifebuoy and Lux. The company is making an effort to boost its margins through the strategy. We do not believe that the price hike will result in a significant boost in sales or margins in the short-term. A large part of the earnings will be spent on promotions and marketing efforts required for relaunches," a dealer at a leading institutional brokerage commented. The HLL stock rose 3.59 per cent to Rs 231 from Rs 223, the third straight day of gains. The personal care wash category accounts for 18 per cent of the company's total sales revenues.

Packaging Functions

- Effective packaging involves more than simply putting products in containers and covering them with wrappers.

- First. packaging materials serve the basic purpose of protecting the product and maintaining its functional form.
- Fluids such as milk and orange juice need packages that preserve and protect them.
- The packaging should prevent damage that could affect the product's usefulness and thus lead to higher costs.
- Since product tampering has become a problem, several packaging techniques have been developed to counter this danger. Some packages are also designed to deter shoplifting.

Another function of packaging is to offer convenience to consumers. For example, small, aseptic packages—individual-size boxes or plastic bags that contain liquids and do not require refrigeration—strongly appeal to children and young adults with active lifestyles.

- The size or shape of a package may relate to the product's storage, convenience of use, or replacement rate.
- Small, single-serving cans of vegetables, for instance, may prevent waste and make storage easier.
- A third function of packaging is to promote a product by communicating its features, uses, benefits, and image.
- Sometimes a reusable package is developed to make the product more desirable. For example, the Cool Whip package doubles as a food-storage container.

Labeling

Labeling is very closely interrelated with packaging and is used for identification, promotional, and informational, and legal purposes. Labels can be small or large relative to the size of the product and carry varying amounts of information. The sticker on a Chiquita banana, for example, is quite small and displays only the brand name of the fruit and perhaps a stock keeping unit number. A label can be part of the package itself or a separate feature attached tothe package. The label on a can of Coke is actually part of the can, whereas the label on a two-liter bottle of Coke is separate and can be removed. Information presented on a label may include the brand name and mark, the registered trademark symbol, package size and content, product features, nutritional information, potential presence of allergens, type and style of the product, number of servings, care instructions, directions for use and safety precautions, the name and address of the manufacturer, expiration dates, seals of approval, and other facts.

Labels can facilitate the identification of a product by displaying the brand name in combination with a unique graphic design. For example, Heinz ketchup is easy to identify on a supermarket shelf because the brand name is easy to read, and the label has a distinctive, crown like shape. By drawing attention to products and their benefits, labels can strengthen an organization's promotional efforts. Labels may contain promotional messages such as the offer of a discount or a larger package size at the same price or information about a new or improved product feature.

MODULE 1.5 PRODUCT LIFE CYCLE

Figure3: Product Life Cycle

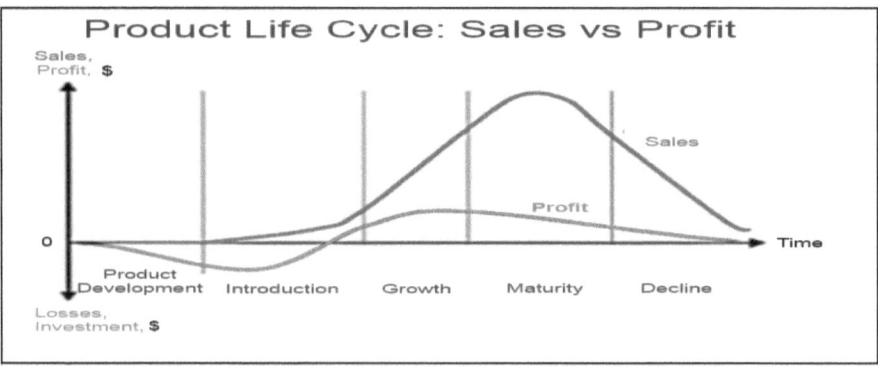

- The **product life cycle** is a ubiquitous in marketing terms, but before we examine its uses and limitations in strategic market planning, we explain the concept.
- The product life cycle proposes that like all life forms, products have finite lives.
- Hence, once a product is introduced to the market it enters a _life cycle'and will eventually fade from the market.

- In addition, the concept proposes that during its life cycle a product will pass through number of different stages, where each stage has characteristic phenomena that suggest specific and different marketing strategies.
- This notion, together with the suggested shape and stages of the _typical'product lifecycle, are shown in Figure.

The characteristics of each stage are:

1 Introduction:

- At this stage the product or service is new to the market.
- The risk of failure is high and any initial sales are likely to be slow. Purchasers at this stage are likely to be innovators who are willing and able to take risks.
- Profit margins are likely to be small or non-existent due to the low volume of sales and high initial launch and marketing costs.
- Money spent during this phase should be regarded as an investment in the future.

2 Growths:

- Provided the product or service meets customer needs and there is a favorable market reaction, sales begin to accelerate as news of the product permeates the market.
- Customers take fewer risks than initial innovator purchasers, but they welcome novelty, and begin to purchase the product.
- Attracted by sales growth and potential profit, new competitors enter the market, often offering variations on the original product to encourage brand loyalty or to avoid patent infringement.

3 Maturities:

Eventually the rate of sales growth will begin to slow down and then cease. A number of factors contribute to this process:

Approaching market saturation: Quite simply, there remain fewer and fewer potential customers left still to purchase the product as it is diffused through the market. Eventually, only replacement sales are made with comparatively few new customers left to purchase for the first time.

Customer boredom/desire for novelty: Customers are fickle when it comes to their appetite for new products. Customers who initially purchased the new product may become bored and switch to other products or brands.

New products/technological change: Successful new products carry within them the seeds of their own destruction. As sales and profits grow, competition is attracted to the market. Often they can only gain entry and market share by developing new or improved versions of the original product. If successful, new products and changes in technology begin to supersede the original product and sales begin to slow.

4 Decline:

- Eventually, forces and factors which contribute to the onset of maturity will erode the market to an extent that sales begin to diminish.
- The rate at which this will occur, and hence length of time the old product will remain viable, varies. Sometimes decline is rapid, as in fashion markets, or when a major technological breakthrough occurs.
- In contrast, the rate of decline may take many years e.g. when a hard core of loyal customers refuse to switch product category or brand.

Different objectives and strategies for each stage

The major use of the product life cycle concept in strategic market planning is based on the notion that characteristics of each stage of the life cycle lend themselves to particular objectives and strategies. We examine this by tracing through each of the stages.

1 Introductory stage

- At this stage, awareness of the new product is low, and competitors are few or nonexistent. Considerable effort may have to be made to bring the product to the attention of distributors and consumers.
- Marketing efforts are likely to be focused on informing customers and promotional and distribution elements of the marketing mix will be targeted at innovator categories.
- Pricing strategies can be aimed either at _skimming'the market through high initial prices that gradually reduce, or at _market penetration', aiming to achieve high levels of market share quickly through low prices.
- Distribution will tend to be exclusive or selective, and advertising aimed at building awareness.

2 Growth stage

- If the new product is successful, we can expect a rapid growth in sales. During this stage new competitors can be expected to enter the market and marketing strategies will need to be focused on combating these new entrants.
- Although price wars are unlikely to develop at this early stage, considerable effort may be required to establish the intensive distribution required for ultimate mass market demand. Communications will be aimed at creating brand image.

3 Maturity stage

- Competition is at its peak. Market share needs defending, while at the same time preserving profit levels. Brand preferences and loyalties are likely to be already established by this stage, but there is likely to be considerable emphasis on trying to encourage brand switching through sales promotion. Price reductions feature here and distribution efforts are aimed at maintaining dealer relationships.

4 Decline stage

- Sales promotion may be reduced to a minimum as the market shrinks. Price competition and price cutting are likely to be intense.
- Emphasis is likely to switch either to looking for ways to extend the product life cycle or to new products, with the old product being _milked'for profits.

Figure4:

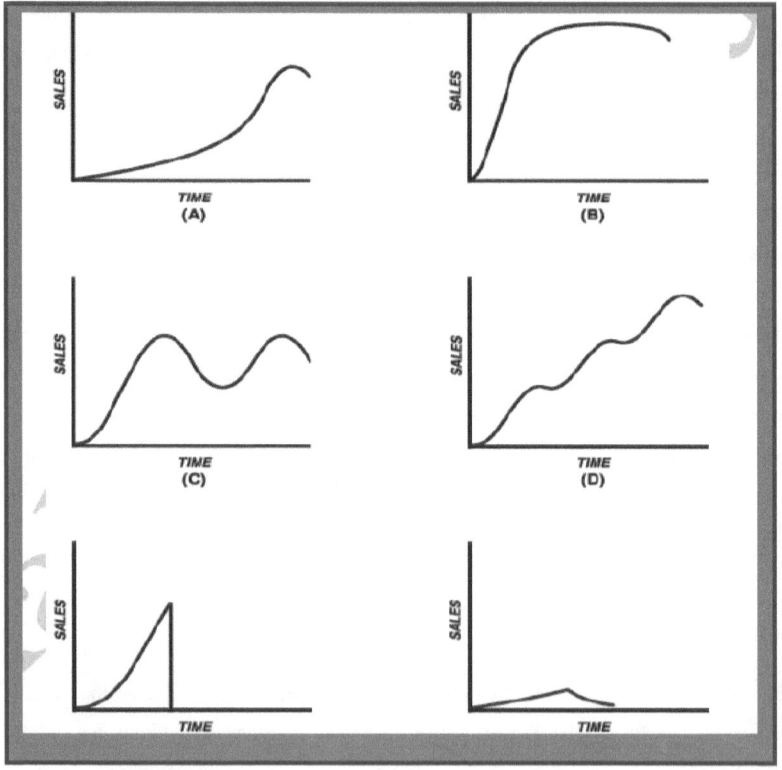

Although typically illustrated as an S-shaped curve, the appearance of the Product Life Cycle varies based on the marketplace experiences of product offerings. Figure 1-2 illustrates six curves that could potentially develop.

Figure 1-2A illustrates the life cycle of a product that witnessed a very lengthy ascent to maturity, possibly because the public was not ready or willing to quickly accept the new offering or perhaps because the entity had difficulties informing the public of the new product's existence. Newly established medical clinics, pharmacies, dental offices, etc. seeking to enter established markets with established providers would likely face this type of life cycle scenarios they strive to develop a customer base.

Figure 1-2B depicts the life cycle of a product that gained immediate acceptance followed by period of enduring maturity. Such a curve would possibly develop upon the discovery of medical breakthrough that was immediately welcomed by customers, such as the discovery of therapeutic intervention for a previously untreatable illness.

Figure 1-2C depicts the life cycle of a product that entered maturity, declined, reentered maturity, and reentered decline. This cyclical pattern would be representative of, for example, medical therapy that experienced provider and patient interest and disinterest over time.

Figure 1-2D illustrates the life cycle of a product that reentered the growth stage multiple times after reaching maturity. Such a curve would be representative of, for example, a pharmaceutical product that was found to be useful for purposes beyond its original scope, resulting in extended growth beyond its initial maturity stage.

Figure 1-2E illustrates the life cycle of a product that experienced a period of rapid growth followed by an immediate decline. This type of curve would be representative of, for example, pharmaceutical product that was suddenly pulled from the market due to newly discovered health concerns. This curve would also be illustrative of a home health agency that was forced to close because of reduced reimbursement rates.

Figure 1-2F illustrates the life cycle of a product that failed after its introduction into the market. This unfortunate life cycle could possibly represent any of the multiple new product offerings that are introduced into the market but fail to achieve commercial success.

CHART NO.1. PRODUCT LIFE CYCLE CHARACTERISTICS AND STRATEGIES

	Introduction	Growth	Maturity	Decline
Users/sales	Few	Increasing rapidly	Settling in	Declining
Costs	High R&D, unit and launch costs	Falling rapidly, utilisation, scale and experience effects	Declining production costs but higher marketing costs	Stabilising
Competitors	Few	New entrants, innovator may sell out	Consolidation	Some exit
Marketing objective	Successful introduction, gain opinion leader endorsement	Build market share by focusing on new customers and creating distinct brand image	Retain customers, get customers to switch, renewals and upgrades, extend life cycle, increase frequency of use, new product uses, cost reduction	Further reduce costs and exploit product or brand
Product	Basic, little variety, quality not high, frequent design changes	Increasing variety and features, good quality and reliability	Stable, standardisation, some tinkering, eg, "new improved xyz"	Declining variety, no further development
Prices	High, price-skimming strategy, introductory offers	Falling slowly, supply constraints may keep prices high	Falling rapidly, discounts, price competition	Stabilising, increasing in late decline stage
Promotion	Promote product, build awareness, user education, press relations, high advertising to sales ratio	Mass-market advertising, increased focus of brand	Focus on brand and its advantages, loyalty, bundling, affinity	Scaled down brand promotion
Place	Specialist retailers, dealers who can give advice, exclusivity deals	Mass-market channels, large multiples	Mass-market channels, large multiples, power of channels increases	Phase out marginal outlets, some multiples may de-list, specialisation
Cash flow	Negative	Break even	Positive	Positive, but declining
Profitability	Losses	Profitable	Margins decline, but offset by volume	Declining margins offset by low depreciation charges, possible write-downs
Risk	High business risk	Low demand side risk, but cash flow risks	Low business risk, cyclical factor impact	Low business risk, labour conflict in unionised industries

<h1>Chapter-2</h1>

Index

UNIT 2 PRICE

Introduction

Pricing is one of the most important decision areas of marketing. Price-fixation is an important managerial function in all business enterprises. If the price set is quite high, the seller may not find enough number of consumers to buy his product. If the price fixed is too low, the seller may not be able to cover his cost. Thus, fixing appropriate price is a major decision-taking function of any enterprise. Price-decisions, no doubt, need to be reviewed from time to time.

MODULE 2.1 PRICING BASICS

Pricing is a fundamental aspect of financial modeling and is one of the four Ps of the marketing mix. The other three aspects are product, promotion, and place. Price is the only revenue generating element amongst the four Ps, the rest being cost centers.

A) Meaning :

Pricing is the process of determining what a company will receive in exchange for its products. Pricing factors are manufacturing cost, market place, competition, market condition, and quality of product. Pricing is also a key variable in micro economic price allocation theory.

B) Definition:

According to Armstrong and Kotler:

"Price is defined as the amount of money charged for a product or service, which the customer has to pay"

Definition - The amount of money charged for a product or service, or the sum of the values that consumers exchange for the benefits of having or using the product or service.

Meaning

- The purpose of marketing is to facilitate satisfying exchange relationships between buyerand seller. **Price** is the value exchanged for products in a marketing transaction.
- Many factors may influence the assessment of value, including time constraints, pricelevels, perceived quality, and motivations to use available information about prices.
- However, price does not always take the form of money paid. In fact, trading of products, or **barter,** is the oldest form of exchange.
- Price is a key element in the marketing mix because it relates directly to the generation of total revenue. The following equation is an important one for the entire organization: Profit = total revenue - total costs

Or

Profits = (price x quantity sold) - total costs

A Black T-Shirt

The black T-shirt for women looks pretty ordinary. In fact, it's not that different from the black T-shirt sold by Gap and by Swedish discount clothing chain H&M. Yet, the Armani T-shirt costs $275.00, whereas the Gap item costs $14.90 and the H&M one $7.90. Customers who purchase the Armani T-shirt are paying for a T-shirt made of 70 percent nylon, 25 percent polyester, and 5 percentelastane, whereas the Gap and H&M shirts are made mainly of cotton. True, the Armani

T is a bit more stylishly cut than the other two and sports a —Made in Italy‖ label, but how does it command a $275.00 price tag? A luxury brand, Armani is primarily known for suits, handbags, and evening gowns that sell for thousands of dollars. In that context, it can sell its T-shirts for more. But because there aren't many takers for $275.00 T-shirts, Armani doesn't make many, thus further enhancing the appeal for status seekers who like the idea of having a —limited edition‖ T-shirt. —Value is not only quality, function, utility, channel of distribution,‖ says Arnold Aronson, managing director of retail strategies for Kurt Salmon Associates and former CEO of Saks Fifth Avenue; it's also a customer's perception of a brand's luxury connotations. 32

Factors Affecting Pricing Decisions

Pricing Objectives :

C) PRICING OBJECTIVES :

1. Survival :
Firm fix low prices for the products. Thus survival objective is a short-term objective.
2. Target Return on Investment :
This is a common objective of well-established and reputed firms in the market to fix a certain rate of return on investment
3. Profit Maximization :
Profit maximization is the age-old objective of pricing. The firm should aim at maximizing profits on total output rather than on each product item.
4. Price Stability :
Many firms have the objective of price stabilization. It is a long-term objective. It is found in industries that have a price leader
5. Market Share :
Market share means that portion of the industry sale, which a firm desire to achieve. The firm may adopt this as an objective either to maintain or to improve the market share.
6. Meet or Prevent Competition :

Price can be used as a weapon to meet the competition or eliminate it. Meeting of competition implies keeping more or less same price as fixed by the competitors.

7. Public Image :

A company's image is important to its success. When a company comes into existence, it develops certain impression in the minds of the people regarding the product quality, package, brand name etc.

8. Cash Recovery :

It may be the pricing objective of some firms to encourage cash sales. Hence, they determine the price for their products to motivate consumers for cash purchases.

9. Skimming The Market Cream :

If the objective of the firm is to skim the market cream, it will fix high price so that the firm can earn maximum profit.

10. Market Penetration :

If the objective of the firm is to restrict the entry of new firms into the market; it adopt market penetration objective.

ORGANIZATIONAL AND MARKETING OBJECTIVES

- Marketers should set prices that are consistent with the organization's goals and mission. For example, a retailer trying to position itself as value-oriented may wish to set pricesthat are quite reasonable relative to product quality.
- In this case a marketer would not want to set premium prices on products but wouldstrive to price products in line with this overall organizational goal.
- Pricing decisions also should be compatible with the organization's marketing objectives.For instance, suppose that one of a producer's marketing objectives is a 12 percentincrease in unit sales by the end of the next year.
- Assuming that buyers are price-sensitive, increasing the price or setting a price above theaverage market price would not be in line with this objective.

TYPES OF PRICING OBJECTIVES

- The types of pricing objectives a marketer uses obviously have considerable bearing on the determination of prices.
- For example, an organization that uses pricing to increase its market share likely wouldset the brand's price below those of competing brands of similar quality to attractcompetitors'customers.
- A marketer sometimes uses temporary price reductions in the hope of gaining marketshare. If a business needs to raise cash quickly, it likely will use temporary pricereductions such as sales, rebates, and special discounts.

COSTS

- Clearly, costs must be an issue when establishing price. A firm temporarily may sell products below cost to match competition, to generate cash flow, or even to increasemarket share, but in the long run it cannot survive by selling its products below cost.
- Even when a firm has a high-volume business, it cannot survive if each item is soldslightly below what it costs.
- A marketer should be careful to analyze all costs so that they can be included in the totalcost associated with a product.
- To maintain market share and revenue in an increasingly price-sensitive market, manymarketers have concentrated on reducing costs.

OTHER MARKETING-MIX VARIABLES

- All marketing-mix variables are highly interrelated. Pricing decisions can influence decisions and activities associated with product, distribution, and promotion variables.
- A product's price frequently affects the demand for that item. Instance, may result in lowunit sales, which, in turn, may lead to higher production costs per unit.
- Conversely, lower per-unit production costs may result from a low price. For manyproducts, buyers associate better product quality with a high price and poorer product
- quality with a low price.
- This perceived price–quality relationship influences customers' overall image of productsor brands. Sony, for example, prices its televisions higher than average to helpcommunicate that Sony televisions are high-quality electronic products.
- Consumers recognize the Sony brand name, its reputation for quality, and the prestigeassociated with buying Sony products.
- Individuals who associate quality with a high price are likely to purchase products with well-established and recognizable brand names.
- The price of a product is linked to several dimensions of its distribution. Premium pricedproducts—a Bentley or a Rolls Royce automobile, for example—are often marketed through selective or exclusive distribution.

Channel Member Expectations

- When making price decisions, a producer must consider what members of the distribution channel expect. A channel member certainly expects to receive a profit for the functions it performs.
- The amount of profit expected depends on what the intermediary could make if it were handling a competing product instead. Also, the amount of time and the resourcesrequired to carry the product influence intermediaries' expectations.
- Channel members often expect producers to give discounts for large orders and promptpayment. At times, resellers expect producers to provide several support activities such assales training, service training, repair advisory service, cooperative advertising, salespromotions, and perhaps a program for returning unsold merchandise to the producer.

These support activities clearly have associated costs that a producer must consider whendetermining prices.

Customer Interpretation and Response
- When making pricing decisions, marketers should be concerned with a vital question:
- How will our customers interpret our prices and respond to them?
- *Interpretation* in this context refers to what the price means or what it communicates to customers.
- Does the price mean —high quality,‖ —low quality,‖ or —great deal,‖ —fair price,‖ or —ripoff‖?
- Customer *response* refers to whether the price will move customers closer to the purchase of the product and the degree to which the price enhances their satisfaction with thepurchase experience and with the product after purchase.

Competition
- A marketer needs to know competitors' prices so that it can adjust its own prices accordingly.
- This does not mean that a company will necessarily match competitors' prices; it may setits price above or below theirs.

- For some organizations, however, matching competitors' prices is an important strategyfor survival.

Legal and Regulatory Issues

- Legal and regulatory issues influence pricing decisions. To curb inflation, thegovernment can invoke price controls, freeze prices at certain levels, or determine therates at which prices may be increased.
- In some states, regulatory agencies set prices on products such as insurance, dairyproducts,
- and liquor.

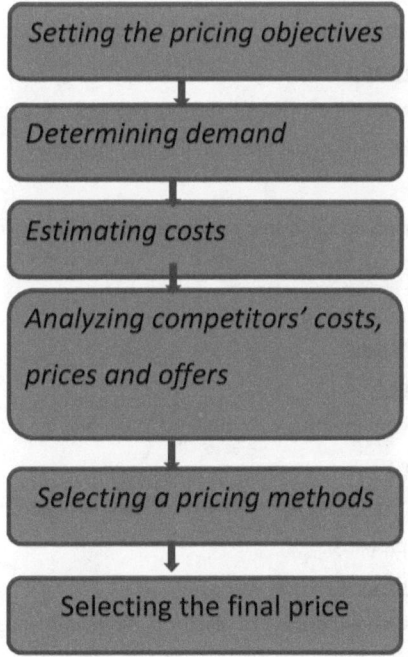

Factors Influencing Pricing Decisions:

Factors Influencing Pricing Decisions:

A) Internal Factors :

Internal factors are those which are within the control of the company. These internal factors affect the pricing decisions of a firm.

1. Costs :

After adding necessary profits with the cost of production it would give the price at which the products

2. Pricing Objectives :

Pricing objectives are overall goals that describe the role of price in the organization's long range plans.

B) External Factors :

External factors are those which are generally beyond the control of the company.

1. Elasticity of Demand :

If the demand increases the price of the product will also increase. On the contrary, if the demand decreases the price of the product will also decrease.

2. Competition :

No manufacturer or producer is free to fix his price without considering competition unless he has a monopoly.

E) Importance of Pricing

1. Essential Element :

Price is a matter of vital importance to both the seller and the buyer in the market place

2. Prime Regulator :

In a free market economy, we have freedom of contract, freedom of enterprise, free competition and right to private property

3. Governs Economic Life :

Economics revolves around pricing of resources. Price influences consumer purchase decisions.

4. Role in Marketing - Mix :

Pricing decision interconnect marketing actions with the financial objectives o

5. Market Share :

Price is typically one of those factors that carry the nearest responsibility for improving or maintaining market share

MODULE 2.2 SETTING THE PRICE

A) Factors to consider when setting price

1. Objectives :

What are the marketing objectives of the firm?

2. Competitors :

Competitor strength influences whether a business can set prices independently, or whether it simply has to follow the normal market price

3. Costs :

A business cannot ignore the cost of production or buying a product when it comes to setting a selling price.

4. The State of the Market for the Product :

If there is a high demand for the product, but a shortage of supply, then the business can put prices up.

5. The State of the Economy :

Some products are more sensitive to changes in unemployment and workers wages than others.

Step 1: Selecting the Pricing Objective

The company first decides where it wants to positionits market offering. The clearer a firm's objectives, theeasier it is to set price. Five major objectives are:survival, maximum current profit, maximum marketshare, maximum market skimming, and productqualityleadership.

SURVIVAL

- Companies pursue *survival* as their majorobjective if they are plagued with overcapacity,
- intense competition, or changing consumer wants.
- As long as prices cover variable costs andsome fixed costs, the company stays in business.
- Survival is a short-run objective; in the longrun, the firm must learn how to add value or face
- extinction.

MAXIMUM CURRENT PROFIT

- Many companies try to set a price that will *maximize current profits.* They estimate the demand and costs associated with alternative prices and choose the price that producesmaximum current profit, cash flow, or rate of return on investment.
- This strategy assumes the firm knows its demand and cost functions; in reality, these aredifficult to estimate.
- In emphasizing current performance, the company may sacrifice long-run performance by ignoring the effects of other marketing variables, competitors' reactions, and legalrestraints on price.

MAXIMUM MARKET SHARE

- Some companies want to *maximize their market share.* They believe a higher sales volume will lead to lower unit costs and higher long-run profit.
- They set the lowest price, assuming the market is price sensitive. Texas Instruments (TI)famously practiced this **market-penetration pricing** for years.

- TI would build a large plant, set its price as low as possible, win a large market share, experience falling costs, and cut its price further as costs fell.

MAXIMUM MARKET SKIMMING

Companies unveiling a new technology favor setting high prices to *maximize market skimming.* Sony is a frequent practitioner of **market-skimming pricing**, in which prices start high andslowly drop over time.

Market skimming makes sense under the following conditions: (1) A sufficient number of buyers have a high current demand; (2) the unit costs of producing a small volume are high enough to cancel the advantage of charging what the traffic will bear; (3) the high initial price does not attract more competitors to the market; (4) the high price communicates the image of a superior product.

PRODUCT-QUALITY LEADERSHIP

A company might aim to be the *product-quality leader* in the market. Many brands strive to be —affordable luxuries‖—products or services characterized by high levels of perceived quality, taste, and status with a price just high enough not to be out of consumers' reach.

Step 2: Determining Demand

- Each price will lead to a different level of demand and have a different impact on a company's marketing objectives.
- The normally inverse relationship between price and demand is captured in a demand curve. The higher the price, the lower the demand. For prestige goods, the demand curvesometimes slopes upward.
- One perfume company raised its price and sold more rather than less! Some consumers take the higher price to signify a better product. However, if the price is too high, demandmay fall.

PRICE SENSITIVITY

The demand curve shows the market's probable purchase quantity at alternative prices. It sums the reactions of many individuals with different price sensitivities. The first step in estimating demand is to understand what affects price sensitivity. Generally speaking, customers are fewer prices sensitive to low-cost items or items they buy infrequently. They are also less price sensitive when

1) there are few or no substitutes or competitors;
2) they do not readily notice the higher price;
3) they are slow to change their buying habits;
4) they think the higher prices are justified; and
5) price is only a small part of the total cost of obtaining, operating, andservicing the product over its lifetime.

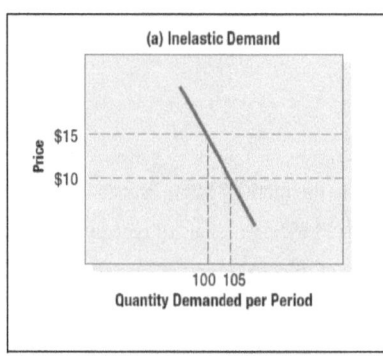

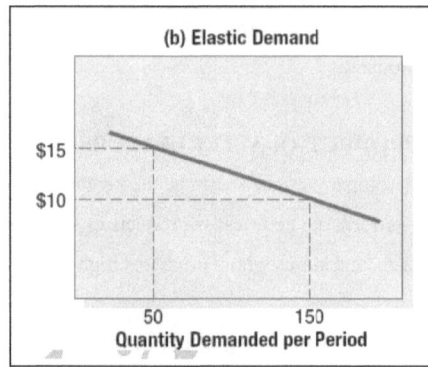

PRICE ELASTICITY OF DEMAND

Marketers need to know how responsive, or elastic, demand is to a change in price. Consider thetwo demand curves in Figure 14.1. In demand curve (a), a price increase from $10 to $15 leads to a relatively small decline in demand from 105 to 100. In demand curve (b), the same price increase leads to a substantial drop in demand from 150 to 50. If demand hardly changes with a small change in price, we say the demand is *inelastic*. If demand changes considerably, demand is *elastic*.

Step 3: Estimating Costs

Demand sets a ceiling on the price the company can charge for its product. Costs set the floor.The company wants to charge a price that covers its cost of producing, distributing, and

sellingthe product, including a fair return for its effort and risk. Yet when companies price products to
cover their full costs, profitability isn't always the net result.

ACCUMULATED PRODUCTION

Suppose TI runs a plant that produces 3,000 hand calculators per day. As TI gains experienceproducing hand calculators, its methods improve. Workers learn shortcuts, materials flow moresmoothly, and procurement costs fall. The result, as Figure shows, is that average cost falls withaccumulated production experience. Thus the average cost of producing the first 100,000 handcalculators is $10 per calculator. When the company has produced the first 200,000 calculators,the average cost has fallen to $9. After its accumulated production experience doubles again t to 400,000, the average cost is $8. This decline in the average cost with accumulated productionexperience is called the **experience curve** or **learning curve**.

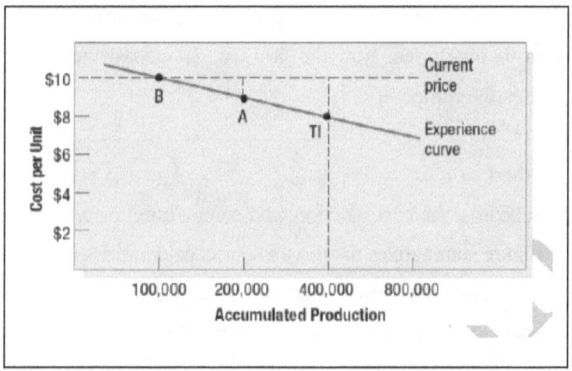

Now suppose three firms compete in this industry, TI, A, and B. TI is the lowest-cost producer at $8, having produced 400,000 units in the past. If all three firms sell the calculator for $10, TI makes $2 profit per unit, A makes $1 per unit, and B breaks even. The smart move for TI would be to lower its price to $9. This will drive B out of the market, and even A may consider leaving. TI will pick up the business that would have gone to B (and possibly A). Furthermore, pricesensitivecustomers will enter the market at the lower price. As production increases beyond400,000 units, TI's costs will drop still further and faster and will more than restore its profits,even at a price of $9. TI has used this aggressive pricing strategy repeatedly to gain market share and drive others out of the industry.

Experience-curve pricing nevertheless carries major risks. Aggressive pricing might give the product a cheap image. It also assumes competitors are weak followers. The strategy leads the company to build more plants to meet demand, but a competitor may choose to innovate with a lower cost technology. The market leader is now stuck with the old technology.

Step 4: Analyzing Competitors' Costs, Prices, and Offers
- Within the range of possible prices determined by market demand and company costs, the firm must take competitors' costs, prices, and possible price reactions into account.
- If the firm's offer contains features not offered by the nearest competitor, it should evaluate their worth to the customer and add that value to the competitor's price.
- If the competitor's offer contains some features not offered by the firm, the firm should subtract their value from its own price. Now the firm can decide whether it can charge more, the same, or less than the competitor.

Step 5: Selecting a Pricing Method
Given the customers' demand schedule, the cost function, and competitors' prices, the company is now ready to select a price. Figure summarizes the three major considerations in price setting: Costs set a floor to the price.Competitors' prices and the price of substitutes provide an orientingpoint. Customers' assessment of unique features establishes the priceceiling.

Companies select a pricing method that includes one or more of thesethree considerations. We will examine six price-setting methods:markup pricing, target-return pricing, perceived-value pricing, valuepricing, going-rate pricing, and auction-type pricing.

MARKUP PRICING
The most elementary pricing method is to add a standard **markup** to the product's cost. Construction companies submit job bids by estimating the total project cost and adding a

standard markup for profit. Lawyers and accountants typically price by adding a standard markup on their time and costs. Variable cost per unit $10Fixed costs $300,000Expected unit sales 50,000Suppose a toaster manufacturer has the following costs and sales expectations:

The manufacturer's unit cost is given by: Unit cost = variable cost + fixed cost = $10 + $30000 = $16Unit sales 50,000Now assume the manufacturer wants to earn a 20 percent markup on sales. The manufacturer's markup price is given by:

Markup price = unit cost = $16 = $20(1 - desired return on sales) 1 - 0.2
The manufacturer will charge dealers $20 per toaster and make a profit of $4 per unit. If dealers Want to earn 50 percent on their selling price; they will mark up the toaster 100 percent to $40. Markups are generally higher on seasonal items (to cover the risk of not selling), specialty items, Slower-moving items, items with high storage and handling costs, and demand-inelastic items, Such as prescription drugs.

TARGET-RETURN PRICING

In **target-return pricing**, the firm determines the price that yields its target rate of return on investment. Public utilities, which need to make a fair return on investment, often use this method. Suppose the toaster manufacturer has invested $1 million in the business and wants to set a price to earn a 20 percent ROE, specifically $200,000. The target-return price is given by the following formula:

Target-return price = unit cost + desired return x invested capital unit sales
= $16 + 0.20 * $1,000,000
50,000
= $20

PERCEIVED-VALUE PRICING

An increasing number of companies now base their price on the customer's **perceived value**.

- Perceived value is made up of a host of inputs, such as the buyer's image of the product performance, the channel deliverables, the warranty quality, customer support, and softer attributes such as the supplier's reputation, trustworthiness, and esteem.

- Companies must deliver the value promised by their value proposition, and the customer must perceive this value.
- Firms use the other marketing program elements, such as advertising, sales force, and the
- Internet, to communicate and enhance perceived value in buyers'minds.

Caterpillar uses perceived value to set prices on its construction equipment. It might price its tractor at $100,000, although a similar competitor's tractor might be priced at $90,000. When a prospective customer asks a Caterpillar dealer why he should pay $10,000 more for the Caterpillar tractor, the dealer answers: $2,000 is the price premium for Caterpillar's longer warranty on parts$110,000 is the normal price to cover Caterpillar's superior value– $10,000 discount$100,000 final price The Caterpillar dealer is able to show that although the customer is asked to pay a $10,000premium, he is actually getting $20,000 extra value! The customer chooses the Caterpillar tractor because he is convinced its lifetime operating costs will be lower.

VALUE PRICING

- In recent years, several companies have adopted **value pricing**: They win loyal customers by charging a fairly low price for a high-quality offering.
- Value pricing is thus not a matter of simply setting lower prices; it is a matter of reengineering the company's operations to become a low-cost producer without sacrificing quality, to attract a large number of value conscious customers.
- Among the best practitioners of value pricing are IKEA, Target, and Southwest Airlines. In the early 1990s, Procter & Gamble created quite a stir when it reduced prices on supermarket staples such as Pampers and Luvs diapers, liquid Tide detergent, and Folgers coffee to value price them.
- To do so, PEG redesigned the way it developed, manufactured, distributed, priced, marketed, and sold products to deliver better value at every point in the supply chain.
- Its acquisition of Gillette in 2005 for $57 billion (a record five times its sales) brought another
- brand into its fold that has also traditionally adopted a value pricing strategy.

GOING-RATE PRICING

- In **going-rate pricing**, the firm bases its price largely on competitors' prices. In oligopolistic industries that sell a commodity such as steel, paper, or fertilizer, all firms normally charge the same price.
- Smaller firms —follow the leader,‖ changing their prices when the market leader's prices change rather than when their own demand or costs change.
- Some may charge a small premium or discount, but they preserve the difference. Thus minor gasoline retailers usually charge a few cents less per gallon than the major oilcompanies, without letting the difference increase or decrease.
- Going-rate pricing is quite popular. Where costs are difficult to measure or competitive response is uncertain, firms feel the going price is a good solution because it is thought to reflect the industry's collective wisdom.

AUCTION-TYPE PRICING
- Auction-type pricing is growing more popular, especially with scores of electronic marketplaces selling everything from pigs to used cars as firms dispose of excess inventories or used goods.

Step 6: Selecting the Final Price

Pricing methods narrow the range from which the company must select its final price. In selecting that price, the company must consider additional factors, including the impact of other marketing activities, company pricing policies, gain-and-risk-sharing pricing, and the impact of price on other parties.

B) Steps in Price Setting:

B) Steps in Price Setting:
Step 1: Selecting the Pricing Objective:

A company can pursue any of five major objectives through pricing: survival, maximum current profit, maximum market share, maximum market skimming, or product-quality leadership

Step 2: Determining Demand :

Each price will lead to a different level of demand and therefore will have a different impact on a company's marketing objectives.

Step 3: Estimating Costs :

Whereas demand sets a ceiling on the price the company can charge for its product, costs set the floor. The company wants to charge a price that covers its cost of producing, distributing, and selling the product, including a fair return for its effort and risk.

Step 4: Analyzing Competitors' Costs, Prices, and Offers :

Within the range of possible prices determined by market demand and company costs, the firm must take into account its competitors' costs, prices, and possible price reactions.

Step 5: Selecting a Pricing Method :

The three Cs-the customers' demand schedule, the cost function, and competitors' prices-are major considerations in setting price.

Types of Pricing

- ➢ Cost Oriented Pricing
- ➢ Competition-Based Approach
- ➢ Marketing Oriented Pricing

Step 6: Selecting the Final Price :

Pricing methods narrow the range from which the company selects its final price. In selecting that price, the company must consider additional factors as belows:

- ➢ Influence of Other Marketing Activities
- ➢ Company Pricing Policies
- ➢ Impact of Price on other Parties
- ➢ Gain-and Risk-Sharing

Problems in Price Setting:

- ➢ Every firm faces problems in setting prices for its products and services.

1. Problem for New Entrant in Setting Price:

> If it sets a high price, it may not generate enough demand. If it sets a low price, it may not be enough to recover costs.

2. Need to Generate Alternative Options :

> The price change may mean a cut in price or increase in the existing price. If it is a price cut then the firm has to react fittingly. Otherwise, the competitor may pull away customers.

3. Compulsive Rate Cut from Profit:

> When circumstances force the initiation of a price cut, a firm has to meet the price cut even if this cuts into profit.

4. Problem in setting Pricing Structure :

> With products that have interrelated costs and use the same raw materials and components, a firm faces the problem of pricing.

MODULE 2.3 ADAPTING THE PRICE

Companies usually do not set a single price but rather develop a pricing structure that reflects variations in geographical demand and costs, market-segment requirements, purchase timing, order levels, delivery frequency, guarantees, service contracts, and other factors. As a result of discounts, allowances, and promotional support, a company rarely realizes the same profit from each unit of a product that it sells.

Geographical Pricing (Cash, Countertrade, Barter)

In geographical pricing, the company decides how to price its products to different customers in different locations and countries. Should the company charge higher prices to distant customers to cover the higher shipping costs, or a lower price to win additional business? How should it account for exchange rates and the strength of different currencies?

Another question is how to get paid. This issue is critical when buyers lack sufficient hard currency to pay for their purchases. Many buyers want to offer other items in payment, a practice known as **countertrade**. Countertrade may account for 15 percent to 20 percent of world trade and takes several forms:

- *Barter.* The buyer and seller directly exchange goods, with no money and no third partyinvolved.
- *Compensation deal.* The seller receives some percentage of the payment in cash and therest in products. A British aircraft manufacturer sold planes to Brazil for 70 percent cashand the rest in coffee.
- *Buyback arrangement.* The seller sells a plant, equipment, or technology to anothercountry and agrees to accept as partial payment products manufactured with the suppliedequipment. A U.S. chemical company built a plant for an Indian company and acceptedpartial payment in cash and the remainder in chemicals manufactured at the plant.
- *Offset.* The seller receives full payment in cash but agrees to spend a substantial amountof the money in that country within a stated time period. PepsiCo sold its cola syrup toRussia for rubles and agreed to buy Russian vodka at a certain rate for sale in the UnitedStates.

Price Discounts and Allowances	
Discount:	A price reduction to buyers who pay bills promptly. A typical example is "2/10, net 30," which means that payment is due within 30 days and that the buyer can deduct 2 percent by paying the bill within 10 days.
Quantity Discount:	A price reduction to those who buy large volumes. A typical example is "$10 per unit for fewer than 100 units; $9 per unit for 100 or more units." Quantity discounts must be offered equally to all customers and must not exceed the cost savings to the seller. They can be offered on each order placed or on the number of units ordered over a given period.
Functional Discount:	Discount (also called *trade discount*) offered by a manufacturer to trade-channel members if they will perform certain functions, such as selling, storing, and record keeping. Manufacturers must offer the same functional discounts within each channel.
Seasonal Discount:	A price reduction to those who buy merchandise or services out of season. Hotels, motels, and airlines offer seasonal discounts in slow selling periods.
Allowance:	An extra payment designed to gain reseller participation in special pro-grams. *Trade-in allowances* are granted for turning in an old item when buying a new one. *Promotional allowances* reward dealers for participating in advertising and sales support programs.

Price Discounts and Allowances

- Most companies will adjust their list price and give discounts and allowances for early payment, volume purchases, and off-season buying.
- Companies must do this carefully or find that their profits are much lower than planned. Discount pricing has become the modus operandi of a surprising number of companies offering both products and services.
- Salespeople, in particular, are quick to give discounts in order to close a sale. But word can get around fast that the company's list price is —soft,‖ and discounting becomes the norm, undermining the value perceptions of the offerings. Some product categories self-destruct by always being on sale.

Promotional Pricing

Companies can use several pricing techniques to stimulate early purchase:

- *Loss-leader pricing:*Supermarkets and department stores often drop the price on wellknownbrands to stimulate additional store traffic. This pays if the revenue on theadditional sales compensates for the lower margins on the loss-leader items.

Manufacturers of loss-leader brands typically object because this practice can dilute the brand image and bring complaints from retailers who charge the list price. Manufacturershave tried to keep intermediaries from using loss-leader pricing through lobbying forretail-price-maintenance laws, but these laws have been revoked.

- *Special event pricing:*Sellers will establish special prices in certain seasons to draw in more customers. Every August, there are back-to-school sales.
- *Special customer pricing:*Sellers will offer special prices exclusively to certaincustomers. Road Runner Sports offers members of its Run America Club —exclusive‖ online offerswith price discounts twice those for regular customers.74
- *Cash rebates:*Auto companies and other consumer-goods companies offer cash rebatesto encourage purchase of the manufacturers' products within a specified time period.

- Rebates can help clear inventories without cutting the stated list price.
- *Low-interest financing:* Instead of cutting its price, the company can offer customers lowinterest financing. Automakers have used no-interest financing to try to attract morecustomers.
- *Longer payment terms:* Sellers, especially mortgage banks and auto companies, stretchloans over longer periods and thus lower the monthly payments. Consumers often worryless about the cost (the interest rate) of a loan, and more about whether they can affordthe monthly payment.
- *Warranties and service contracts:* Companies can promote sales by adding a free or lowcost
- warranty or service contract.
- *Psychological discounting:* This strategy sets an artificially high price and then offers theproduct at substantial savings; for example, —Was $359, now $299.‖ Discounts fromnormal prices are a legitimate form of promotional pricing; the Federal TradeCommission and Better Business Bureaus fight illegal discount tactics.

DIFFERENTIATED PRICING

Companies often adjust their basic price to accommodate differences in customers, products, locations, and so on. Lands‘ End creates men‘s shirts in many different styles, weights, and levels of quality.

Price discrimination occurs when a company sells a product or service at two or more prices that do not reflect a proportional difference in costs. In first-degree price discrimination, the seller charges a separate price to each customer depending on the intensity of his or her demand. In second-degree price discrimination, the seller charges less to buyers of larger volumes. With certain services such as cell phone service, however, tiered pricing results in consumers paying *more* with higher levels of usage. With the iPhone, 3 percent of users accounted for 40 percent of the traffic on AT&T‘s network, resulting in costly network upgrades.

In third-degree price discrimination, the seller charges different amounts to different classes of buyers, as in the following cases:

- *Customer-segment pricing:*Different customer groups pay different prices for the sameproduct or service. For example, museums often charge a lower admission fee to students and senior citizens.
- *Product-form pricing:*Different versions of the product are priced differently, but not proportionately to their costs. Evian prices a 48-ounce bottle of its mineral water at $2.00
- and 1.7 ounces of the same water in a moisturizer spray at $6.00.
- *Image pricing:*Some companies price the same product at two different levels based on image differences. A perfume manufacturer can put the perfume in one bottle, give it asame and image, and price it at $10 an ounce. The same perfume in another bottle with a different name and image and price can sell for $30 an ounce.
- *Channel pricing:*Coca-Cola carries a different price depending on whether the consumerpurchases it in a fine restaurant, a fast-food restaurant, or a vending machine.
- *Location pricing:*The same product is priced differently at different locations even though the cost of offering it at each location is the same. A theater varies its seat pricesaccording to audience preferences for different locations.
- *Time pricing:*Prices are varied by season, day, or hour. Public utilities vary energy rates to commercial users by time of day and weekend versus weekday. Restaurants chargeless to —early bird‖ customers, and some hotels charge less on weekends.

MODULE 2.4 - PRICE CHANGE

Initiating and Responding to Price Changes

Companies often need to cut or raise prices. Initiating Price Cuts Several circumstances might lead a firm to cut prices. One is *excess plant capacity*: The firm needs additional business and cannot generate it through increased sales effort, product improvement, or other measures. Companies sometimes initiate price cuts in a *drive to dominate the market through lower costs.*

Either the company starts with lower costs than its competitors, or it initiates price cuts in the hope of gaining market share and lower costs.

A price-cutting strategy can lead to other possible traps:

- **Low-quality trap:**Consumers assume quality is low.
- **Fragile-market-share trap :**A low price buys market share but not market loyalty. The same customers will shift to any lower-priced firm that comes along.
- **Shallow-pockets trap:**Higher-priced competitors match the lower prices but have longer staying power because of deeper cash reserves.
- **Price-war trap:**Competitors respond by lowering their prices even more, triggering a price war.Customers often question the motivation behind price changes. They may assume the item isabout to be replaced by a new model; the item is faulty and is not selling well; the firm is in financial trouble; the price will come down even further; or the quality has been reduced. The firm must monitor these attributions carefully.

Initiating Price Increases

A successful price increase can raise profits considerably. If the company's profit margin is 3 percent of sales, a 1 percent price increase will increase profits by 33 percent if sales volume is unaffected. This situation is illustrated in Table 14.6. The assumption is that a company charged $10 and sold 100 units and had costs of $970, leaving a profit of $30, or 3 percent on sales. By raising its price by 10 cents (a 1 percent price increase), it boosted its profits by 33 percent, assuming the same sales volume.

A major circumstance provoking price increases is *cost inflation*. Rising costs unmatched by productivity gains squeeze profit margins and lead companies to regular rounds of price increases.

Companies often raise their prices by more than the cost increase, in anticipation of further inflation or government price controls, in a practice called *anticipatory pricing*.

Another factor leading to price increases is *over demand*. When a company cannot supply all its customers, it can raise its prices, ration supplies, or both. It can increase price in the following ways, each of which has a different impact on buyers.

Chapter-3

Index

UNIT 3 PLACE

MODULE 3.1 THE ROLE OF MARKETING CHANNELS

The manufactured products must reach the customer so that his wants are fulfilled. Channels of distribution are paths through which products move from the points of production to the points of consumption. The channel design should be such that it will ensure speedy, timely delivery not burden the company financially. Of late, Logistics is given utmost importance. Logistics is the process of designing, managing, and improving the movement of products through the supply chain. Logistics has the objective of delivering exactly what the customer wants—at the right time, in the right place, and at the right price. In logistics, the focus is on the customer.

Meaning :

A channel of distribution or trade channel is path or route along which goods move from producers or manufacturers to ultimate consumers or industrial users.

A channel of distribution consists of three types of flows :
- ➤ Downward flow of goods from producers to consumers
- ➤ Upward flow of cash payments for goods from consumers to producers
- ➤ Flow of marketing information in both downward and upward direction

B) Definitions :

As per Cundiff, Still and Govani :

"A channel of Distribution or Marketing Channels are the distribution networks through which producers products flow to the market."

As per William J. Stanton :

"This is a route taken by the title to the goods as they move from producer to the ultimate consumers or industrial users."

Figure : **Factors Affecting Choice of Marketing Channels :**

Factors Affecting Choice of Marketing Channels :

1. Market Considerations :

A logical starting point is to consider the target market its needs, structure and buying behavior, in the following order:
- ➤ Type of Market
- ➤ Number of Potential Customers
- ➤ Geographic Concentration of the Market
- ➤ Order Size

2. Product Considerations :

a) Unit Value :

The price attached to each unit of product affects the amount of funds available for distribution

b) Perishability :

Some products have a very short shelf life and so have to be sold through short distribution channels.

c) Technical Nature of the Product :

A business product that is highly technical is often distributed directly

3. Middleman Considerations :

Why should we consider the need to have middlemen? The reasons may be the followings:

- ➤ **Services Provided by Middlemen**
- ➤ **Availability of Desired Middlemen**
- ➤ **Attitude of Middlemen Towards Producer's Policies**

4. Company Considerations :

Before choosing a distribution channel of a product, a company should also consider its own situation, i.e. conduct a SWOT analysis of its resources.

- ➤ **Desire or Channel Control**
- ➤ **Services Provided by Seller**
- ➤ **Ability of Management**
- ➤ **Financial Resources**
- ➤ **Marketing Channel Functions :**

- ➤ **1. Transactional Functions:**

- ➤ *These transactional functions include buying, selling and risk bearing functions. The channels also minimize transaction costs.*

- ➤ **2. Logistical Functions:**

- ➤ *The channels of distribution perform logistical functions, which are involved in the physical exchange of goods. These logistical functions include assembling, storage, grading and transportation.*

- ➤ **3. Facilitating Functions:**

- ➤ *The channels of distribution perform facilitating functions like after sales service and maintenance, financing and market information etc.*

- ➤ **4. Utility Creation:**

➤ *The channels of distribution create place utility by facilitating the movement of goods from one place to another. The channels of distribution create time utility by bringing the goods to the consumers when they want*

➤ **_Marketing Channel Flows :_**

➤ **_1. Information Flow :_**

➤ *Meaningful communications among channel participants depend on transmission of useful and informative facts and data. The information flow is a two-way exchange of useful information between two parties within one or more channel settings.*

➤ **_2. Promotional Flow:_**

➤ *The promotional flow is a firm's presentation of persuasive communications directed at influencing the behaviors of customers (final consumer promotions) and other channel participants (trade promotions).*

➤ **_3. Negotiations Flow:_**

➤ *The interplay of sellers and buyers within the marketing exchange process encompasses the negotiation flow. Negotiation has been described as the art of give and take, where discussions are directed at resolving differences and issues*

➤ **_4. Transaction Flow:_**

➤ *Order placement and fulfillment constitute the two key activities of the transaction flow.*

A marketing channel (also called a channel of distribution or distribution channel) is a group of individuals and organizations that directs the flow of products from producers to customers.

- The major role of marketing channels is to make products available at the right time, at the right place, and in the right quantities.
- Providing customer satisfaction should be the driving force behind marketing-channel decisions. Buyers' needs and behavior are therefore important concerns of channel members.
- Some marketing channels are direct, meaning that the product goes directly from the producer to customer.
- For example, when a customer orders a laptop from Dell, this product is sent from the manufacturer to the customer.

- Most channels, however, have marketing intermediaries. A **marketing intermediary** (or *middleman*) links producers to other intermediaries or to ultimate consumers through contractual arrangements or through the purchase and reselling of products.
- Marketing intermediaries can perform most marketing activities.
- For example, eBay serves as a marketing intermediary between Internet sellers and buyers.
- Wholesalers and retailers are examples of intermediaries.
- Wholesalers buy and resell products to other wholesalers, to retailers, and to industrial customers.
- Retailers purchase products and resell them to ultimate consumers.

Fig: Using Intermediaries to Streamline the Number of Transactions

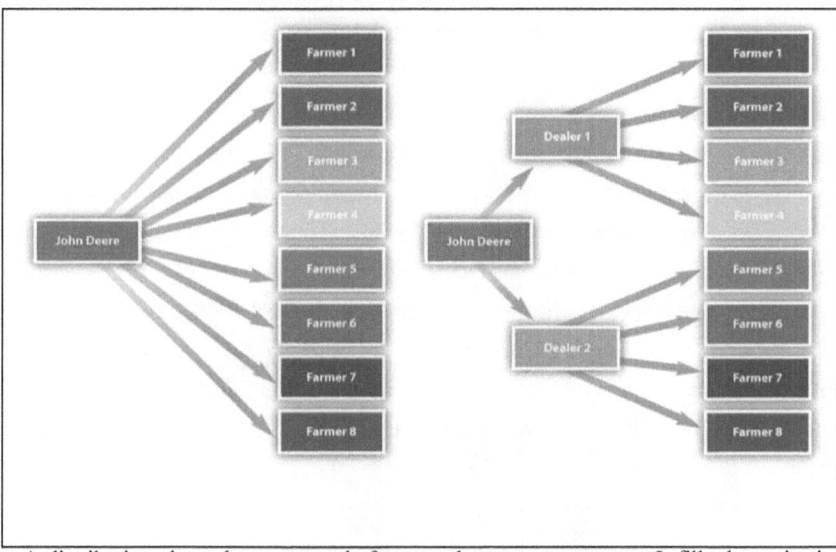

A distribution channel moves goods from producers to consumers. It fills the main time, place and possession gaps that separate goods and services from those who would use them. Members of the marketing channel perform many key functions. Some help to complete transactions:

1. Information: Gathering and distributing marketing research and intelligence information about actors and forces in the marketing environment needed for planning and facilitating exchange.

2. Promotion: Developing and spreading persuasive communications about an offer.

3. Contact: Finding and communicating with prospective buyers.

4. Matching; Shaping and fitting the offer to the buyer's needs, including such activities as manufacturing, grading, assembling and packaging.

5. Negotiation- Reaching an agreement on price and other terms of die offer, so that ownership or possession can be transferred.

Others help to fulfill the completed transactions:

6. Physical distribution- Transporting and storing goods.

7. Financing- Acquiring and using funds to cover the costs of the channel work.

8. Risk taking- Assuming the risks of carrying out the channel work.

Philips Royal Philips Electronics of the Netherlands is one of the world's biggest electronics companies and Europe's largest, with sales of over $66 billion in 2009. Philips's electronics products are channeled toward the consumer primarily through local and international retailers. The company offers a broad range of products from high to low price/value quartiles, relying on a diverse distribution model that includes mass merchants, retail chains, independents, and small specialty stores. To work most effectively with these retail channels, Philips has created an organization designed around its retail customers, with dedicated global key account managers serving leading retailers such as Best Buy, Carrefour, Costco, Dixons, and Tesco. Like many modern firms, Philips also sells via the Web through its own online store as well as through a number of other online retailers.

TYPES OF MARKETING CHANNELS

The various marketing channels can be classified generally as channels for consumer products and channels for business products.

1. **Consumer Products**

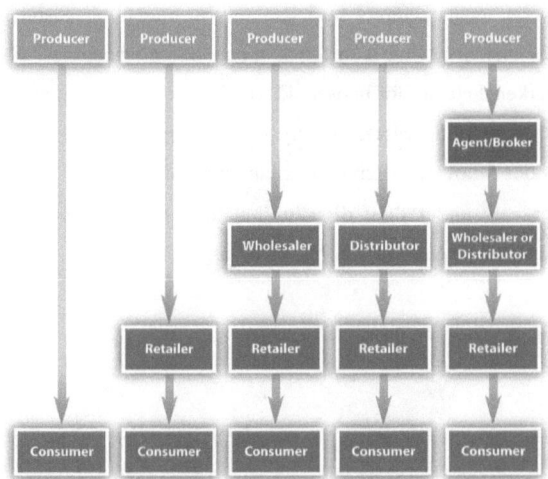

2. Business Products

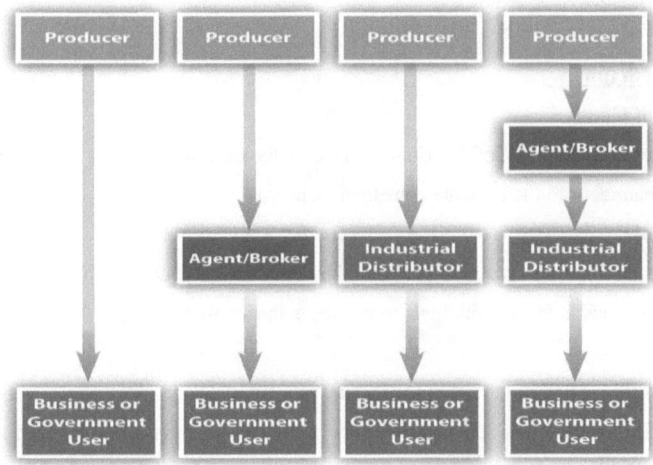

3. Multiple Marketing Channels and Channel Alliances

- To reach diverse target markets, manufacturers may use several marketing channels simultaneously, with each channel involving a different group of intermediaries. For example, when Del Monte markets ketchup for household use, it is sold to supermarkets through grocery wholesalers or, in some cases, directly to retailers, whereas ketchup going to restaurants or institutions follows a different distribution channel.
- In some instances a producer may prefer **dual distribution,** the use of two or more marketing channels to distribute the same products to the same target market.

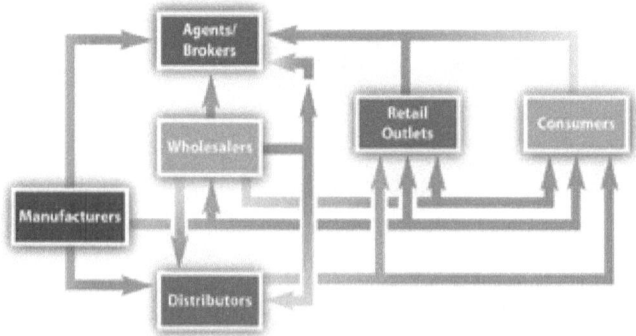

Roles of Marketing Channels :

1. Transfer of Title of Goods :

The important role of the channels of distribution is transfer of title of goods from one channel to the next channel or to the ultimate consumer or user.

2. Merchandising Role:

Merchandising role is an important function performed by the distribution channels. Through merchandising, the channels help the principals to reinforce the awareness about the product among the customers

3. Providing Distributional Efficiency to Manufacturers :

The channels bring together the marketers and the users in an efficient and economic manner.

4. Communication of Information :

The channels of distribution provide information to the consumers concerning the availability, characteristics and price of the goods

MODULE 3.2 CHANNEL DESIGN DECISIONS

It consists of the following steps:

1. Analyzing customer service needs.
2. Defining the channel objectives and constraints.
3. Identifying the major channel alternatives.
4. Evaluating those alternatives.

Steps in channel design:

---

1. Analyzing customer service needs

Like most marketing decisions, designing a channel begins with the customer. Marketing channels are viewed as customer *value delivery* systems in which each channel member adds value for the customer Thus designing the distribution channel starts with finding out what *values* consumers in various target segments want from the channel.

- Do customers want to buy from nearby locations or are they willing to travel to more centralized locations?
- Would they rather buy in person or over the phone or through the mail?
- Do they want immediate delivery or are they willing to wait?
- Do they value breadth of assortment or do they prefer specialization?

- Do customers want many add-on services (delivery, credit, repairs, installation) or will they obtain these elsewhere?

2. Defining the channel objectives and constraints

- Channel objectives should be stated in terms of the desired service level of target customers. Usually, a company can identify several segments wanting different levels of channel service. The company should decide which segments to serve and the best channels to use in each ease. In each segment, the company wants to minimize the totalm channel cost of supplying customers, while also meeting their service requirements.
- The company's channel objectives are also influenced by the nature of its products, company policies, marketing intermediaries, competitors and the environment.
- *Product characteristics* greatly affect channel design. For example, perishable products require more direct marketing to avoid delays and too much handling. Bulky products, such as building materials and soft drinks, require channels chat minimize shipping distance and the amount of handling.
- *Company characteristics* also play an important role. For example, the company's size and financial situation determine which marketing functions it can handle itself and which it must give to intermediaries.
- Furthermore, a company marketing strategy based on speedy customer delivery affects the functions that the company wants its intermediaries to perform, the number of its outlets and the choice of its transportation methods.

3. Identifying the major channel alternatives

Having defined its channel objectives, the firm then identifies its major channel alternatives in terms of the *types* and *number* of intermediaries to *use* and the *responsibilities* of each channel member.

Types of Alternative Channel

A number of options exist:

a) **Direct marketing**

A number of direct marketing approaches can be used, ranging from direct-response selling via advertisements in print media, on radio or television, by mail order and catalogues to telephone and Internet selling.

b) Sales force

The company can sell directly through its own *sales force* or deploy another firm's sales force, as Glaxo did with its best-selling anti-ulcer drug. Zantac. Alternatively, a contract sales force might be used.

c) Intermediaries

These arc independent organizations that will carry out a number of activities. *Merchants,* which include wholesalers and retailers, buy, take title to and resell the firm's goods, whereas brokers and agents do not buy or carry the producer's products, but help to sell these to customers by negotiating prices and sales terms and conditions on the supplier's behalf. Other intermediaries - transport companies, independent warehouses, finance companies, banks - perform a range of channel functions to facilitate the flow of goods or services from producer to user.

4. Evaluating those alternatives

- Suppose a company has identified several channel alternatives and wants to select the one that will best satisfy its long-run objectives.
- The firm must evaluate each alternative against economic, control and adaptive criteria. Using economic criteria, the company compares the likely profitability of different channel alternatives. It estimates the sales that each channel would produce and the costs of selling different volumes through each channel.
- The company must also consider control issues. Using intermediaries usually means giving them some control over the marketing of the product, and some intermediaries take more control than others.
- Other things being equal, the company prefers to keep as much control as possible. Finally, the company must apply adaptive criteria. Channels often involve long-term commitments to other firms and loss of flexibility, making it hard to adapt the channel to a changing marketing environment. The producer wants to keep the channel as flexible as possible.

MODULE 3.3 CHANNEL OPTIONS
RETAILING
Meaning:
Retailing is the sale of goods in small quantities to ultimate consumers. The word retailer is of French origin meaning "to cut again".
Definition:
- William J. Stanton:

"Retailing includes all activities directly related to the sale of goods and services to the ultimate consumers for personal and non-business use."
Functions:
- Buying and Assembling Goods
- Arranging Storage
- Grading and Packaging
- Sales Promotion
- Physical Distribution

- **Retailing** includes all transactions in which the buyer intends to consume the product through personal, family, or household use.
- Buyers in retail transactions are therefore the ultimate consumers.
  A **retailer** is an organization that purchases products for the purpose of reselling them to ultimate consumers.
- Although most retailers' sales are made directly to the consumer, nonretail transactions occur occasionally when retailers sell products to other businesses.
- Retailing often takes place in stores or service establishments, but it also occurs through direct selling, direct marketing, and vending machines outside stores.

Table : General Merchandise Retailers

Type of Retailer	Description
Department store	Large organization offering wide product mix and organized into separate departments
Discount store	Self-service general merchandise store offering brand name and private brand products at low prices
Convenience store	Small self-service store offering narrow product assortment in convenient locations
Supermarket	Self-service store offering complete line of food products and some nonfood products
Superstore	Giant outlet offering all food and nonfood products found in supermarkets, as well as most routinely purchased products
Hypermarket	Combination supermarket and discount store; larger than a superstore
Warehouse club	Large-scale members-only establishments combining cash-and-carry wholesaling with discount retailing
Warehouse showroom	Facility in a large, low-cost building with large on-premises inventories and minimal service

Department Stores

- **Department stores** are large retail organizations characterized by wide product mixes and organized into separate departments, such as cosmetics, housewares, apparel, home furnishings, and appliances, to facilitate marketing and internal management.
- Often each department functions as a self-contained business, and buyers for individual departments are fairly autonomous.

Discount Stores

- In recent years, department stores have been losing market share to discount stores.
- **Discount stores** are self-service general merchandise outlets that regularly offer brand name and private brand products at low prices.
- Discounters accept lower margins than conventional retailers in exchange for high sales volume. To keep inventory turnover high, they carry a wide but carefully selected assortment of products, from appliances to housewares and clothing.
- Most operate in large (50,000 to 80,000 square feet), facilities.

Convenience Stores

- A **convenience store** is a small self-service store that is open long hours and carries a narrow assortment of products, usually convenience items such as soft drinks and other beverages, snacks, newspapers, tobacco, and gasoline, as well as services such as automatic teller machines.
- The primary product offered by the —corner store‖ is convenience.
- They are typically less than 5,000 square feet; open 24 hours a day, 7 days a week, and stock about 500 items.

Supermarkets

- **Supermarkets** are large self-service stores that carry a complete line of food products, as well as some nonfood products such as cosmetics and nonprescription drugs. Supermarkets are arranged in departments for maximum efficiency in stocking and handling products but have central checkout facilities.

- They offer lower prices than smaller neighborhood grocery stores, usually provide free parking, and also may cash checks.
- Today, consumers make more than three-quarters of all grocery purchases in supermarkets.

Superstores

- **Superstores**, which originated in Europe, are giant retail outlets that carry not only food and nonfood products ordinarily found in supermarkets but also routinely purchased consumer products.
- Superstores combine features of discount stores and supermarkets.
- Examples include Wal-Mart Supercenters and some Kroger stores. Besides a complete food line, superstores sell housewares, hardware, small appliances, clothing, personal care products, garden products, and tires—about four times as many items as supermarkets.
- Superstores can have an area of as much as 200,000 square feet (compared with 20,000 square feet in traditional supermarkets).

Hypermarkets

- **Hypermarkets** combine supermarket and discount store shopping in one location. Larger than superstores, they range from 225,000 to 325,000 square feet and offer 45,000 to 60,000 different types of low-priced products.
- They commonly allocate 40 to 50 percent of their space to grocery products and the remainder to general merchandise, including athletic shoes, designer jeans, and other apparel; refrigerators, televisions, and other appliances; housewares; cameras; toys; jewelry; hardware; and automotive supplies.
- Many lease space to noncompeting businesses such as banks, optical shops, and fast-food restaurants.

Warehouse Clubs

- **Warehouse clubs,** a rapidly growing form of mass merchandising, are large-scale members-only selling operations combining cash-and-carry wholesaling with discount retailing.
- Sometimes called buying clubs, warehouse clubs offer the same types of products as discount stores but in a limited range of sizes and styles.

- Whereas most discount stores carry around 40,000 items, a warehouse club handles only 3,500 to 5,000 products, usually acknowledged brand leaders.

Warehouse Showrooms
- **Warehouse showrooms** are retail facilities with five basic characteristics: large, low-cost buildings; warehouse materials-handling technology; vertical merchandise displays; large on-premises inventories; and minimal services.
- IKEA, a Swedish company, sells furniture, household goods, and kitchen accessories in warehouse showrooms and through catalogs around the world, including China and Russia.

Specialty Retailers
- In contrast to general merchandise retailers with their broad product mixes, specialty retailers emphasize narrow and deep assortments.
- Despite their name, specialty retailers do not sell specialty items (except when specialty goods complement the overall product mix).
- Instead, they offer substantial assortments in a few product lines.
- There are three types of specialty retailers: traditional specialty retailers, category killers, and off-price retailers.

Traditional specialty retailers
- **Traditional specialty retailers** are stores that carry a narrow product mix with deep product lines. Sometimes called limited-line retailers, they may be referred to as singleline retailers if they carry unusual depth in one main product category.
- Traditional specialty retailers commonly sell shopping products such as apparel, jewelry, sporting goods, fabrics, computers, toys, and pet supplies.
- The Limited, Radio Shack, Hickory Farms, The Gap, and Foot Locker are examples of retailers offering limited product lines but great depth within those lines.
- Many traditional specialty retailers are small businesses with just one or a few outlets.

Category Killer

- Over the last 15 years, a new breed of specialty retailer, the category killer, has evolved.
- A **category killer** is a very large specialty store that concentrates on a major product category and competes on the basis of low prices and enormous product availability.
- These stores are referred to as category killers because they expand rapidly and gain sizable market shares, taking business away from smaller, high-cost retail outlets.
- Examples of category killers include Home Depot and Lowe's (home improvement chains); Staples, Office Depot, and OfficeMax (office-supply chains); Borders and Barnes & Noble (booksellers); Petco and PetSmart (pet-supply chains); and Best Buy and Circuit City (consumer electronics).

Off-price retailers

- **Off-price retailers** are stores that buy manufacturers' seconds, overruns, returns, and offseason production runs at below-wholesale prices for resale to consumers at deep discounts.
- Unlike true discount stores, which pay regular wholesale prices for goods and usually carry second-line brand names, off-price retailers offer limited lines of national-brand and designer merchandise, usually clothing, shoes, or housewares.

FRANCHISING

Meaning:

Franchising is a long-term cooperative relationship between two entities—a franchisor and one or more franchisees—that is based on an agreement in which the franchisor provides a licensed privilege to the franchisee to do business.

Benefits of franchising

- ➢ **Provides Well Established Profitable Business**
- ➢ **Pre-opening Benefits**
- ➢ **Overall Competitive Benefits**
- ➢ **Ongoing Benefits**

- **Franchising** is an arrangement in which a supplier, or franchiser, grants a dealer, or franchisee, the right to sell products in exchange for some type of consideration.
- The franchiser may receive some percentage of total sales in exchange for furnishing equipment, buildings, management know-how, and marketing assistance to the franchisee.
- The franchisee supplies labor and capital, operates the franchised business, and agrees to abide by the provisions of the franchise agreement.

WHOLESALING

Meaning:

Wholesaling is the set of all activities involved in selling goods and/ or services to those buying for resale or business use.

Definition:

- Cundiif and Still:

"Wholesalers buy and resell merchandise to retailers 'and other merchants and to industrial, institutional and commercial users, but do not sell in significant amounts to ultimate consumers."

Functions of Wholesaler:

- Buying and Assembling
- Selling
- Warehousing
- Transportation
- Financing

- **Wholesaling** refers to all transactions in which products are bought for resale, for making other products, or for general business operations. It does not include exchanges with ultimate consumers.
- A **wholesaler** is an individual or organization that sells products that are bought for resale, for making other products, or for general business operations.
- In other words, wholesalers buy products and resell them to reseller, government, and institutional users.
- Wholesaling activities are not limited to goods; service companies, such as financial institutions, also use active wholesale networks.

- For example, some banks buy loans in bulk from other financial institutions, as well as making loans to their own retail customers.
- Wholesalers may engage in many supply-chain management activities, including warehousing, shipping and product handling, inventory control, information system management and data processing, risk taking, financing, budgeting, and even marketing research and promotion.

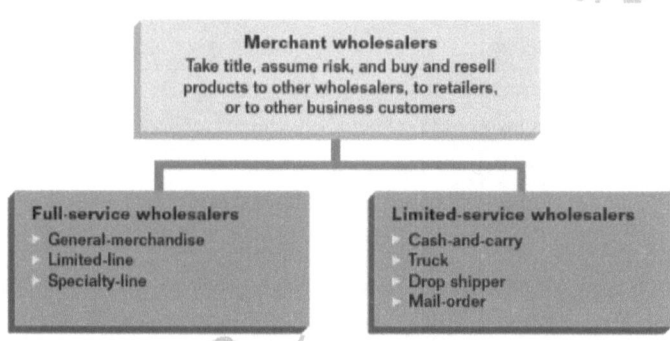

Types of Wholesalers

Wholesalers are classified according to several criteria. Whether a wholesaler is independently owned or owned by a producer influences how it is classified.

1. Merchant wholesalers Independently owned businesses that take title to goods, assume ownership risks, and buy and resell products to other wholesalers, business customers, or retailers.

a) Full-service wholesalers- Merchant wholesalers that perform the widest range of wholesaling functions

   I.   **General merchandise wholesalers-** Full-service wholesalers with a wide product mix but limited depth within product lines

  II.   **General-line wholesalers-** Full-service wholesalers that carry only a few product lines but many products within those lines

 III.   **Specialty-line wholesalers-** Full-service wholesalers that carry only a single product line or a few items within a product line

IV. **Rack jobbers-** Full-service, specialty- line wholesalers that own and maintain display racks in stores

b) Limited-service wholesalers- Merchant wholesalers that provide some services and specialize in a few functions

i. **Cash-and-carry wholesalers-** Limited-service wholesalers whose customers pay cash and furnish transportation

ii. **Truck wholesalers-** Limited-service wholesalers that transport products directly to customers for inspection and selection

iii. **Drop shippers-** Limited-service wholesalers that take title to products and negotiate sales but never take actual possession of products

iv. **Mail-order wholesalers-** Limited- service wholesalers that sell products through catalogs

Table : Service that limited –service whole-salers provide

	Cash-and-Carry	Truck	Drop Shipper	Mail-Order
Physical possession of merchandise	Yes	Yes	No	Yes
Personal sales calls on customers	No	Yes	No	No
Information about market conditions	No	Some	Yes	Yes
Advice to customers	No	Some	Yes	No
Stocking and maintenance of merchandise in customers' stores	No	No	No	No
Credit to customers	No	No	Yes	Some
Delivery of merchandise to customers	No	Yes	No	No

2. Agents- Intermediaries that represent either buyers or sellers on a permanent basis

a) **Manufacturers' agents-** Independent intermediaries that represent two or more sellers and offer complete product lines

b) **Selling agents-** Intermediaries that market a whole product line or a manufacturer's entire output

c) **Commission merchants-** Agents that receive goods on consignment and negotiate sales in large, central markets

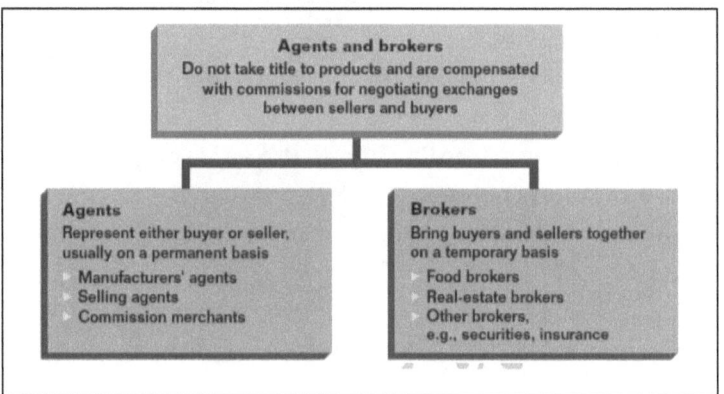

4. Brokers Intermediaries that bring buyers and sellers together temporarily

Table : Service that Agent and Broker Provides

	Manufacturers' Agents	Selling Agents	Commission Merchants	Brokers
Physical possession of merchandise	Some	Some	Yes	No
Long-term relationship with buyers or sellers	Yes	Yes	Yes	No
Representation of competing product lines	No	No	Yes	Yes
Limited geographic territory	Yes	No	No	No
Credit to customers	No	Yes	Some	No
Delivery of merchandise to customers	Some	Yes	Yes	No

4. Manufacturers' Sales Branches and Offices- Sometimes called manufacturers' wholesalers, manufacturers' sales branches and offices resemble merchant wholesalers' operations.

a) **Sales branches-** Manufacturer owned intermediaries that sell products and provid support services to the manufacturer's sales force

b) **Sales offices-** Manufacturer owned operations that provide services normally associated with agents

DIRECT MARKETING

Meaning:

Direct marketing is an interactive system of marketing, which uses one or more advertising media to affect a measurable response and transaction at any location.

Definition:

- The Direct Marketing Association:

"An interactive form of marketing using one or more advertising media to affect a measurable response and/or transaction at any location, with this activity stored on database."

Benefits:

➢ Facilitates Relations Building

➢ Cost Effective

➢ Versatile Form of Marketing

➢ Measurability

➢ Flexibility

Direct marketing is the use of telecommunications and nonpersonal media to communicate product and organizational information to customers, who then can purchase products via mail, telephone, or the Internet. Direct marketing can occur through catalog marketing, direct response marketing, telemarketing, television home shopping, and online retailing.

Catalog Marketing

- In **catalog marketing**, an organization provides a catalog from which customers make selections and place orders by mail, telephone, or the Internet. The advantages of catalog retailing include efficiency and convenience for customers. The retailer benefits by being able to locate in remote, low-cost areas; save on expensive store fixtures; and reduce both personal selling and store operating expenses.

- On the other hand, catalog retailing is inflexible, provides limited service, and is most effective for a selected set of products.

Direct Response Marketing

- **Direct response marketing** occurs when a retailer advertises a product and makes it available through mail or telephone orders.
- Generally, a purchaser may use a credit card, but other forms of payment are acceptable.
- Examples of direct response marketing include a television commercial offering a recording artist's musical collection available through a toll-free number, a newspaper or magazine advertisement for a series of children's books available by filling out the form in the ad or calling a toll-free number.
- Direct response marketing is also conducted by sending letters, samples, brochures, or booklets to prospects on a mailing list and asking that they order the advertised products by mail or telephone.

Telemarketing

- A number of organizations use the telephone to strengthen the effectiveness of traditional marketing methods.
- **Telemarketing** is the performance of marketing-related activities by telephone. Some organizations use a prescreened list of prospective clients.
- Telemarketing can help to generate sales leads, improve customer service, speed up payments on past-due accounts, raise funds for nonprofit organizations, and gather marketing data.

Television Home Shopping

- **Television home shopping** presents products to television viewers, encouraging them to order through toll-free numbers and pay with credit cards.
- The Home Shopping Network in Florida originated and popularized this format.
- The most popular products sold through television home shopping are jewelry (40 percent of total sales), clothing, housewares, and electronics.
- The television home shopping format offers several benefits.

- Products can be demonstrated easily, and an adequate amount of time can be spent showing the product so that viewers are well informed.
- The length of time a product is shown depends not only on the time required for doing demonstrations but also on whether the product is selling.
- Once the calls peak and begin to decline, a new product is shown.
- Other benefits are that customers can shop at their convenience and from the comfort of their homes.

E-Commerce Marketing Concepts

Meaning:

The term "Electronic Commerce" (or e-commerce) refers to the use of an electronic medium to carry out commercial transactions

Definition:

Ravi Kalakota:

"From a communications perspective, electronic commerce is the delivery of information, products/ services, or payments via telephone lines, computer networks, or any other means."

Benefits:

➢ **Providing Information**
➢ **Online Buying / Selling**
➢ **Improved Supplier-Customer Relationships**
➢ **Quicker Delivery**
➢ **Increased Potential Market Share**

MODULE 3.4 MARKET LOGISTICS DECISIONS

Meaning:

Logistics is the management of the flow of resources between the point of origin and the point of consumption in order to meet some requirements, for example, of customers or corporations. The resources managed in logistics can include physical items, such as food, materials, equipment, liquids, and staff, as well as abstract items, such as time, information, particles, and energy.

B) Definitions:

- **Philip Kotler:**

"Planning, implementing, and controlling the physical flows of materials and finished goods from point of origin to point of use to meet the customer's need at a profit."

- **Bowersox and Closs :**

"Logistics management includes the design and administration of systems to control the flow of materials, work in progress and finished inventory to support business unit strategy."

Market logistics includes planning the infrastructure to meet demand, then implementing and controlling the physical flows of materials and final goods from points of origin to points of use, to meet customer requirements at a profit. Market logistics planning has four steps:

- Deciding on the company's value proposition to its customers. (What on-time delivery standard should we offer? What levels should we attain in ordering and billing accuracy?)
- Selecting the best channel design and network strategy for reaching the customers. (Should the company serve customers directly or through intermediaries? What products should we source from which manufacturing facilities? How many warehouses should we maintain and where should we locate them?)
- Developing operational excellence in sales forecasting, warehouse management, transportation management, and materials management
- Implementing the solution with the best information systems, equipment, policies, and procedures.
- Studying market logistics leads managers to find the most efficient way to deliver value. For example, a software company might traditionally produce and package software disks and manuals, ship them to wholesalers, which ship them to retailers, which sell them to customers, who bring them home to download onto their PCs. Market logistics offers two superior delivery systems. The first lets the customer download the software directly onto his or her computer. The second allows the computer manufacturer to download the software onto its products. Both solutions eliminate the need for printing, packaging, shipping, and stocking millions of disks and manuals.

OBJECTIVES OF LOGISTIC SYSTEM :

1. Improving Customer Service :

An important objective of all marketing efforts, including the physical distribution activities, is to improve the customer service.

2. Rapid Response :

Rapid response is concerned with a firm's ability to satisfy customer service requirements in a timely manner.

3. Reduce Total Distribution Costs :

The objective of the firm should be to reduce the total cost of distribution and not just the cost incurred on any one element.

4. Generating Additional Sales :

Another important objective of the physical distribution / logistics system in a firm is to generate additional sales. A firm can attract additional customers by offering better services at lowest prices

Significance of Logistic System :

1. Assurance of Satisfaction :

Logistics management ensures the highest level of customer service and satisfaction by achieving the right combination of product availability and dependability.

2. Minimization of Costs :

It minimizes the opening costs of physical materials system

3. Enhancement in Form of Possession :

It adds place and enhances the form and possession value added by manufacturing and marketing.

4. Reduction in Time :

It reduces time spent at every stage of the chain from procurement to delivery to customer.

5. Image Building

It helps in raising company's image and improves its competitive position in the market.

Scope of Logistic System :

1. Customer Service :

Customer service acts as the binding and unifying force for all of the logistics management activities. Each component of the logistics system can affect, whether a customer receives the right product at the right place, in the right condition, for the right cost at the right time.

2. Physical Distribution :

Physical distribution is the set of activities concerned with efficient movement of finished goods from the end of the production operation to the consumer.

3. Materials Management :

Materials management can deal with campus planning and building design for the movement of materials, or with logistics that deal with the tangible components of a supply chain.

4. Supply Chain Management :

Supply chain management (SCM) is the management of a network of interconnected businesses involved in the provision of product and service packages required by the end customers in a supply chain.

MARKET-LOGISTICS DECISIONS

The firm must make four major decisions about its market logistics:

1. How should we handle orders (order processing)?
2. Where should we locate our stock (warehousing)?
3. How much stock should we hold (inventory)? and
4. How should we ship goods (transportation)?

ORDER PROCESSING

- Most companies today are trying to shorten the *order-to-payment cycle*—that is, the elapsed time between an order's receipt, delivery, and payment.
- This cycle has many steps, including order transmission by the salesperson, order entry and customer credit check, inventory and production scheduling, order and invoice shipment, and receipt of payment.
- The longer this cycle takes, the lower the customer's satisfaction and the lower the company's profits.

WAREHOUSING

- Every company must store finished goods until they are sold, because production and consumption cycles rarely match.
- On the one hand, more stocking locations mean goods can be delivered to customers more quickly, but warehousing and inventory costs are higher.
- To reduce these costs, the company might centralize its inventory in one place and use fast transportation to fill orders.
- Some inventory is kept at or near the plant, and the rest in warehouses in other locations. The company might own private warehouses and also rent space in public warehouses.
  - *Storage warehouses* store goods for moderate to long periods of time.
  - *Distribution warehouses* receive goods from various company plants and suppliers and move them out as soon as possible.
  - *Automated warehouses* employ advanced materials-handling systems under the control of a central computer and are increasingly becoming the norm.
- Some warehouses are now taking on activities formerly done in the plant. These include assembly, packaging, and constructing promotional displays.
- Postponing finalization of the offering to the warehouse can achieve savings in costs and finer matching of offerings to demand.

INVENTORY

- Salespeople would like their companies to carry enough stock to fill all customer orders immediately. However, this is not cost-effective.

- Management needs to know how much sales and profits would increase as a result of carrying larger inventories and promising faster order fulfillment times, and then make a decision.
- As inventory draws down, management must know at what stock level to place a new order. This stock level is called the *order (or reorder) point.* An order point of 20 means reordering when the stock falls to 20 units. The order point should balance the risks of stock-out against the costs of overstock. The other decision is how much to order. The larger the quantity ordered, the less frequently an order needs to be placed. The company needs to balance order-processing costs and inventory-carrying costs.
- *Order-processing costs* for a manufacturer consist of *setup costs* and *running costs* (operating costs when production is running) for the item. If setup costs are low, the manufacturer can produce the item often, and the average cost per item is stable and equal to the running costs. If setup costs are high, however, the manufacturer can reduce the average cost per unit by producing a long run and carrying more inventory.
- Order-processing costs must be compared with *inventory-carrying costs.* The larger the average stock carried, the higher the inventory-carrying costs. These carrying costs include storage charges, cost of capital, taxes and insurance, and depreciation and obsolescence. Carrying costs might run as high as 30 percent of inventory value. This means that marketing managers who want their companies to carry larger inventories need to show that the larger inventories would produce incremental gross profits to exceed incremental carrying costs.

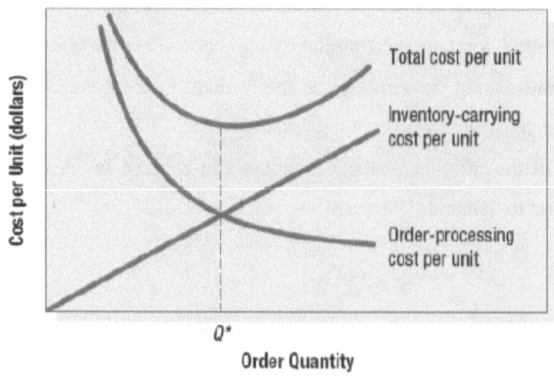

- The ultimate answer to carrying *near-zero inventory* is to build for order, not for stock.
- Sony calls it SOMO, —Sell one, make one.
- Dell's inventory strategy for years has been to get the customer to order a computer and pay for it in advance. Then Dell uses the customer's money to pay suppliers to ship the necessary components.
- As long as customers do not need the item immediately, everyone can save money. Some retailers are unloading excess inventory on eBay where, by cutting out the traditional liquidator middleman, they can make 60 to 80 cents on the dollar as opposed to 10 cents. And some suppliers are snapping up excess inventory to create opportunity.

TRANSPORTATION

- Transportation choices affect product pricing, on-time delivery performance, and the condition of the goods when they arrive, all of which affect customer satisfaction.
- In shipping goods to its warehouses, dealers, and customers, the company can choose rail, air, truck, waterway, or pipeline. Shippers consider such criteria as speed, frequency, dependability, capability, availability, traceability, and cost. For speed, air, rail, and truck are the prime contenders. If the goal is low cost, then the choice is water or pipeline.
- Shippers are increasingly combining two or more transportation modes, thanks to containerization.
- **Containerization** consists of putting the goods in boxes or trailers that are easy to transfer between two transportation modes. *Piggyback* describes the use of rail and trucks; *fishyback*, water and trucks; *trainship*, water and rail; and *airtruck*, air and trucks.
- Each coordinated mode offers specific advantages. For example, piggyback is cheaper than trucking alone yet provides flexibility and convenience.
- Shippers can choose private, contract, or common carriers. If the shipper owns its own truck or air fleet, it becomes a *private carrier.*
- A *contract carrier* is an independent organization selling transportation services to others on a contract basis. A *common carrier* provides services between predetermined points on a scheduled basis and is available to all shippers at standard rates.
- **Material Handling and Storage System:**

- The speed of the inventory movement across the supply drain depends on the material handling methods. An improper method of material handling will add to the product damages and delays in deliveries and incidental overheads. Mechanization and automation in material handling enhance the logistics system productivity.

6. Logistical Packaging :

- Logistical or industrial packaging is a critical element in the physical distribution of a product which influences the efficiency of the logistical system. It differs from product packaging, which is based on marketing objectives.

7. Information:

- Logistics is basically an information-based activity of inventory movement across a supply chain. Hence, an information system plays a vital role in delivering a superior service to the customers.

	4.1 Introduction: The role of marketing communications in marketing effort.
	4.2 Communication Mix Elements: Introduction to Advertising, Sales Promotion, Personal Selling, Public Relations, Direct Marketing. Concept of Integrated Marketing Communications (IMC)
	4.3 Developing Effective Communication: Identifying target audience, determining communication objectives, designing the communications, selecting communication channels
	4.4 Deciding Marketing Communications Mix: Factors in setting marketing communication mix, measuring communication results

MODULE 4.1 INTRODUCTION

Modern marketing calls for more than developing a good product, pricing it attractively, and making it accessible. Companies must also communicate with present and potential stakeholders as well as the public. The marketing communications mix consists of advertising, sales promotion, public relations and publicity, personal selling, and direct marketing, although savvy marketers know that communication goes beyond these methods. The product's styling and price, the package's shape and color, the salesperson's manner and dress, the place's decor—all communicate something to buyers.

- **Marketing communications** are the means by which firms attempt to inform, persuade, and remind consumers—directly or indirectly—about the products and brands they sell.

- Marketing communications also work for consumers when they show how and why a product is used, by whom, where, and when. Consumers can learn who makes the product and what the company and brand stand for, and they can get an incentive for trial or use.

- Marketing communications allow companies to link their brands to other people, places, events, brands, experiences, feelings, and things.

Meaning:

Marketing Communications is the process to inform, persuade, remind and influence consumers or users in favor of particular product or service.

B) Definition :

- **Philip Kotler :**

"A company's total marketing communication mix - also called its promotion mix consists of the specific blend of advertising, personal selling, sales promotion, public relations and direct marketing tools that the company uses to pursue its advertising and marketing objectives."

C) Objectives :

- ➤ Build Awareness
- ➤ Create Interest
- ➤ Provide Information
- ➤ Stimulate Demand
- ➤ Reinforce the Brand

Definition - Promotion mix

The specific mix of advertising, personal setting, sales promotion and public relations that a company uses to pursue its advertising and marketing objectives.

What Is Integrated Marketing Communications?

- **Integrated marketing communications (IMC)** refers to the coordination of promotional efforts to ensure maximum informational and persuasive impact on customers. Coordinating multiple marketing tools to produce this synergistic effect requires a marketer to employ a broad perspective. A major goal of integrated marketing communications is to send a consistent message to customers.

- Communication is essentially the transmission of information. For communication to take place, both the sender and the receiver of information must share some common ground. They must have a common understanding of the symbols, words, and pictures used to transmit information.

- Thus we define **communication** as a sharing of meaning.

- Implicit in this definition is the notion of transmission of information because sharing necessitates transmission.

- As Figure shows, communication begins with a source.

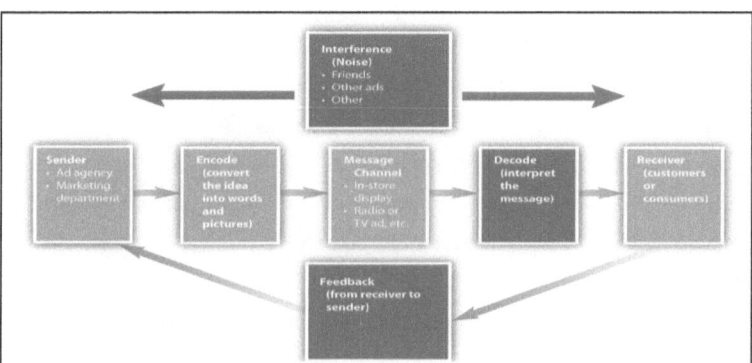

ROLE OF COMMUNICATION

1. Create Awareness

- A considerable amount of promotion focuses on creating awareness. For an organization introducing a new product or a line extension, making customers aware of the product is crucial to initiating the product adoption process.
- A marketer that has invested heavily in product development strives to create product awareness quickly to generate revenues to offset the high costs of product development and introduction. To create awareness of its new Spicy Premium Chicken sandwich, for example, McDonald's passed out samples of the sandwich, coupons, T-shirts, and iPod covers in 14 cities.

2. Stimulate Demand

- When an organization is the first to introduce an innovative product, it tries to stimulate **primary demand**—demand for a product category rather than for a specific brand of product—through pioneer promotion.
- **Pioneer promotion** informs potential customers about the product: what it is, what it does, how it can be used, and where it can be purchased. Because pioneer promotion is used in the introductory stage of the product life cycle, which means there are no competing brands, it

neither emphasizes brand names nor compares brands. The first company to introduce the digital video recorder, for instance, initially attempted to stimulate primary demand by emphasizing the benefits of digital video recorders in general rather than the benefit of its specific brand.

3. Encourage Product Trial

- When attempting to move customers through the product adoption process, a marketer may successfully create awareness and interest, but customers may stall during the evaluation stage.
- In this case, certain types of promotion, such as free samples, coupons, test drives or limited free-use offers, contests, and games, are employed to encourage product trial. For Example, Bru usually gives free trials of their coffee mix in various cities.

4. Identify Prospects

- Certain types of promotional efforts are directed at identifying customers who are interested in the firm's product and are most likely to buy it.
- A marketer may use a magazine advertisement with a direct-response information form, requesting the reader to complete and mail the form to receive additional information.
- Some advertisements have toll-free numbers to facilitate direct customer response. Customers who fill out information blanks or call the organization usually have higher interest in the product, which makes them likely sales prospects. The organization personal contact by salespeople.

5. Retain Loyal Customers

- Clearly, maintaining long-term customer relationships is a major goal of most marketers. Such relationships are quite valuable.
- Promotional efforts directed at customer retention can help an organization control its costs because the costs of retaining customers are usually considerably lower than those of acquiring new ones.
- Frequent-user programs, such as those sponsored by airlines, car rental agencies, and hotels, seek to reward loyal customers and encourage them to remain loyal.

6. Facilitate Reseller Support

- Reseller support is a two-way street. Producers generally want to provide support to resellers to maintain sound working relationships, and in turn, they expect resellers to support their products.
- When a manufacturer advertises a product to consumers, resellers should view this promotion as a form of strong manufacturer support.
- In some instances, a producer agrees to pay a certain proportion of retailers' advertising expenses for promoting its products.
- When a manufacturer is introducing a new consumer brand in a highly competitive product category, it may be difficult to persuade supermarket managers to carry this brand.

7. Combat Competitive Promotional Efforts

- At times, a marketer's objective in using promotion is to offset or lessen the effect of a competitor's promotional program.
- This type of promotional activity does not necessarily increase the organization's sales or market share, but it may prevent a sales or market share loss.
- A combative promotional objective is used most often by firms in extremely competitive consumer markets, such as the fast-food and automobile industries.

8. Reduce Sales Fluctuations

- Demand for many products varies from one month to another because of factors such as climate, holidays, and seasons.
- When promotional techniques reduce fluctuations by generating sales during slow periods, a firm can use its resources more efficiently.
- Promotional techniques are often designed to stimulate sales during sales slumps.

Push and Pull Channel Policies

Another element marketers consider when planning a promotion mix is whether to use a push policy or a pull policy.

Push Policy

- With a **push policy**, the producer promotes the product only to the next institution down the marketing channel. In a marketing channel with wholesalers and retailers, the producer promotes to the wholesaler because in this case the wholesaler is the channel member just below the producer (see Figure). Each channel member, in turn, promotes to the next channel member. A push policy normally stresses personal selling. Sometimes sales promotion and advertising are used in conjunction with personal selling to push the products down through the channel.

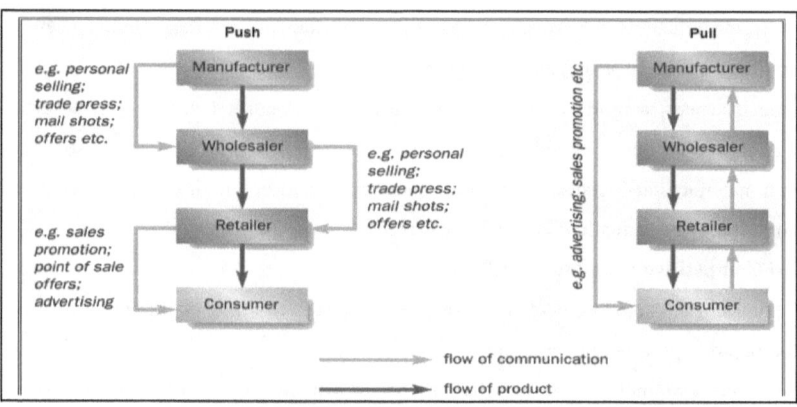

Pull Policy

- As Figure shows, a firm using a **pull policy** promotes directly to consumers to develop strong consumer demand for its products.
- It does so primarily through advertising and sales promotion. Because consumers are persuaded to seek the products in retail stores, retailers, in turn, go to wholesalers or the producers to buy the products.
- This policy is intended to pull the goods down through the channel by creating demand at the consumer level.
- Consumers are told that if the stores don't have it, ask them to get it. Push and pull policies are not mutually exclusive. At times, an organization uses both simultaneously.

MODULE 4.2 COMMUNICATION MIX ELEMENTS

Integration of all the elements of promotion mix is necessary to meet the information requirements of all target customers. This simply means that the promotion mix is not designed to satisfy only the prospective buyer or only the regular buyer.

PROMOTIONAL ELEMENT	MASS VERSUS CUSTOMIZED	PAYMENT	STRENGTHS	WEAKNESSES
Advertising	Mass	Fees paid for space or time	• Efficient means for reaching large numbers of people	• High absolute costs • Difficult to receive good feedback
Personal selling	Customized	Fees paid to salespeople as either salaries or commissions	• Immediate feedback • Very persuasive • Can select audience • Can give complex information	• Extremely expensive per exposure • Messages may differ between salespeople
Public relations	Mass	No direct payment to media	• Often most credible source in the consumer's mind	• Difficult to get media cooperation
Sales promotion	Mass	Wide range of fees paid, depending on promotion selected	• Effective at changing behavior in short run • Very flexible	• Easily abused • Can lead to promotion wars • Easily duplicated
Direct marketing	Customized	Cost of communication through mail, telephone, or computer	• Messages can be prepared quickly • Facilitates relationship with customer	• Declining customer response • Database management is expensive

ADVERTISING

Advertising :

Meaning :

Advertising is a form of communication for marketing and used to encourage, persuade, or manipulate an audience (viewers, readers or listeners; sometimes a specific group) to continue or take some new action.

Definitions :

AccordiWilliam J. Stanton :

"Advertising consists of all the activities involved in presenting to an audience a non-personal, sponsor-identified, paid-for message about a product or organization."

- **Webstar :**

"Advertising is to give public notice or to announce publicity".

C) Features of Advertising

- ➢ Communication
- ➢ Information
- ➢ Profit Maximization
- ➢ Element of Creativity

Advertising is a paid form of non-personal communication transmitted to a target audience through mass media, such as television, radio, the Internet, newspapers, magazines, direct mail, outdoor displays, and signs on mass transit vehicles.

- When asked to name major advertisers, most people immediately mention business organizations.
- However, many non-business types of organizations, including governments, churches, universities, and charitable organizations, employ advertising to communicate with stakeholders.
- Advertising is used to promote goods, services, ideas, images, issues, people, and anything else that advertisers want to publicize or foster.

Developing an Advertising Campaign

An **advertising campaign** involves designing a series of advertisements and placing them in various advertising media to reach a particular target audience.

1. Identifying and Analyzing the Target Audience

- The **target audience** is the group of people at whom advertisements are aimed.
- Advertisements for Barbie cereal are targeted toward young girls who play with Barbie dolls, whereas those for Special K cereal are directed at health-conscious adults.
- Identifying and analyzing the target audience are critical actions.
- The information yielded helps to determine other steps in developing the campaign.

The target audience for a campaign may include everyone in the firm's target market or only a portion of the target market.

2. Defining the Advertising Objectives

- The advertiser's next step is to determine what the firm hopes to accomplish with the campaign.
- Because advertising objectives guide campaign development, advertisers should define objectives carefully.
- Advertising objectives should be stated clearly, precisely, and in measurable terms.
- Precision and measurability allow advertisers to evaluate advertising success at the end of the campaign in terms of whether or not objectives have been met.

3. Creating the Advertising Platform

- Before launching a political campaign, party leaders develop a political platform stating the major issues that are the basis of the campaign.
- Like a political platform, an **advertising platform** consists of the basic issues or selling points that an advertiser wishes to include in the advertising campaign.
- An advertising platform should consist of issues important to customers. One of the best ways to determine those issues is to survey customers about what they consider most important in the selection and use of the product involved.
- Selling features must not only be important to customers, but they also should be strongly competitive features of the advertised brand.

4. Determining the Advertising Appropriation

- The **advertising appropriation** is the total amount of money a marketer allocates for advertising for a specific time period.
- It is hard to decide how much to spend on advertising for a specific period because the potential effects of advertising are so difficult to measure precisely.
- Many factors affect a firm's decision about how much to appropriate for advertising.
- Geographic size of the market and the distribution of buyers within the market have a great bearing on this decision.
- Of the many techniques used to determine the advertising appropriation, one of the most logical is the **objective-and-task approach**. Using this approach, marketers determine the objectives a campaign is to achieve and then attempt to list the tasks required to accomplish them. The costs of the tasks are calculated and added to arrive at the total appropriation. A coffee marketer, for example, may find it extremely difficult to determine how much of an increase in television advertising is needed to raise a brand's market share from 8 to 10 percent.
- In the more widely used **percent-of-sales approach**, marketers simply multiply the firm's past sales, plus a factor for planned sales growth or decline, by a standard percentage based on what the firm traditionally spends on advertising and perhaps on the industry average. This approach is flawed because it is based on the incorrect assumption that sales create advertising rather than the reverse. A marketer using this approach during declining sales will reduce the amount spent on advertising, but such a reduction may further diminish sales. Though illogical, this technique has been used widely because it is easy to implement.
- Another way to determine the advertising appropriation is the **competition matching approach**. Marketers following this approach try to match their major competitors' appropriations in absolute dollars or to allocate the same percentage of sales for advertising that their competitors do.

5. Developing the Media Plan

- To derive maximum results from media expenditures, marketers must develop effective media plans. A **media plan** sets forth the exact media vehicles to be used (specific magazines, television stations, newspapers, and so forth) and the dates and times the advertisements will appear.

- The plan focuses on how many people in the target audience will be exposed to a message and the frequency of exposure. To formulate a media plan, the planners select the media for the campaign and prepare a time schedule for each medium. The media planner's primary goal is to reach the largest number of people in the advertising target audience that the budget will allow.

6. Creating the Advertising Message

- The basic content and form of an advertising message are functions of several factors. A product's features, uses, and benefits affect the content of the message.
- Characteristics of the people in the target audience—gender, age, education, race, income, occupation, lifestyle, and other attributes—influence both content and form.

7. Executing the Campaign

- Execution of an advertising campaign requires extensive planning and coordination because many tasks must be completed on time and many people and firms are involved.
- Production companies, research organizations, media firms, printers, photoengravers, and commercial artists are just a few of the people and firms contributing to a campaign.

8. Evaluating Advertising Effectiveness

- Advertising can be evaluated before, during, and after the campaign. An evaluation performed before the campaign begins is called a **pretest**.
- A pretest usually attempts to evaluate the effectiveness of one or more elements of the message.
- To pretest advertisements, marketers sometimes use a **consumer jury**, a panel of actual or potential buyers of the advertised product. Jurors judge one or several dimensions of two or more advertisements.
- Such tests are based on the belief that consumers are more likely than advertising experts to know what influences them.

Advertising :

D) Importance of Advertising :

- ➤ Promotion of Sales
- ➤ Introduction of New Product

- ➤ Creation of Good Public Image
- ➤ Research
- ➤ Education to People
- ➤ Makes the Job Easy for Salesman

E) Limitations of Advertising

- ➤ Misleading Claims
- ➤ Encourage Monopoly
- ➤ Buying Problems
- ➤ Misuse of Advertising
- ➤ Promotion of Social Evil

PUBLIC RELATIONS

- **Public relations** are a broad set of communication efforts used to create and maintain favorable relationships between an organization and its stakeholders.
- An organization communicates with various stakeholders, both internal and external, and public relations efforts can be directed toward any and all of these.
- A firm's stakeholders can include customers, suppliers, employees, stockholders, the media, educators, potential investors, government officials, and society in general.
- Public relations can be used to promote people, places, ideas, activities, and even countries. It focuses on enhancing the image of the total organization.
- Assessing public attitudes and creating a favorable image are no less important than direct promotion of the organization's products.
- Because the public's attitudes toward a firm are likely to affect the sales of its products, it is very important for firms to maintain positive public perceptions.

Public Relations Tools
Publicity

- Publicity is part of public relations. **Publicity** is communication in news-story form about the organization, its products, or both transmitted through a mass medium at no charge.
- For example, after Apple chairman Steve Jobs announced that the company would introduce a revolutionary new mobile phone, the iPhone, the story was covered in newspapers and television news shows throughout the world for months afterward.

- Although public relations has a larger, more comprehensive communication function than publicity, publicity is a very important aspect of public relations.
- Publicity can be used to provide information about goods or services; to announce expansions, acquisitions, research, or new product launches; or to enhance a company's image.

News / Press Release

- The most common publicity-based public relations tool is the **news release**, sometimes called a *press release,* which is usually a single page of typewritten copy containing fewer than 300 words and describing a company event or product.
- A news release gives the firm's or agency's name, address, phone number, and contact person. News releases can tackle a multitude of specific issues.

Feature Article

- A **feature article** is a manuscript of up to 3,000 words prepared for a specific publication.

Captioned Photograph

- A **captioned photograph** is a photograph with a brief description explaining the picture's content.
- Captioned photographs are effective for illustrating new or improved products with highly visible features.

Press Conference

- A **press conference** is a meeting called to announce major news events.
- Media personnel are invited to a press conference and are usually supplied with written materials and photographs.
- Letters to the editor and editorials are sometimes prepared and sent to newspapers and magazines.
- Videos and audiotapes may be distributed to broadcast stations in the hope that they will be aired.

PERSONAL SELLING

Personal Selling:

A) Meaning:

Personal selling refers to the direct selling. It includes face-to-face communication. This can be done by "Knocking on Doors", by setting up meetings, over the telephone, organizing conferences, workshops.

B) Definition:

Haughton :

"Salesmanship is personal service rendered to the community in connection with marketing of goods."

C) Methods of Personal Selling:

- Across the Counter Selling
- Door-to-Door Selling

D) Benefits of Personal Selling

- Personal Communication
- Increasing Sales
- Quick Feedback
- **Personal selling** is paid personal communication that attempts to inform customers and persuade them to purchase products in an exchange situation.
- For example, a salesperson describing the benefits of a Toyota Innova to a customer at a dealership is engaging in personal selling. Personal selling goals vary from one firm to another.
- However, they usually involve finding prospects, persuading prospects to buy, and keeping customers satisfied.
- Personal selling gives marketers the greatest freedom to adjust a message so that it will satisfy customers' information needs.
- Compared with other promotion methods, personal selling is the most precise, enabling marketers to focus on the most promising sales prospects.
- Other promotion-mix elements are aimed at groups of people, some of whom may not be prospective customers. However, personal selling is generally the most expensive element in the promotion mix.

Personal Selling Process

1. Prospecting for Customers

- Developing a list of potential customers is called **prospecting**. Salespeople seek names of prospects from company sales records, trade shows, commercial databases, newspaper
- announcements (of marriages, births, deaths, and so on), public records, telephone directories, trade association directories, and many other sources.
- Sales personnel also use responses to traditional and online advertisements that encourage interested persons to send in information request forms.
- Seminars and meetings targeted at particular types of clients, such as attorneys or accountants, also may produce leads.
- Most salespeople prefer to use referrals—recommendations from current customers— to find prospects.
- Obtaining referrals requires that the salesperson have a good relationship with the current customer and so must have performed well before asking the customer for help.

2. Evaluating Prospects

- Before contacting acceptable prospects, a salesperson finds and analyzes information about each prospect's specific product needs, current use of brands, feelings about available brands, and personal characteristics.
- In short, salespeople need to know what potential buyers and decision makers consider most important and why they need a specific product.
- The most successful salespeople are thorough in their evaluations of prospects.

3. Approaching the Customer

- The **approach**, the manner in which a salesperson contacts a potential customer, is a critical step in the sales process.
- In more than 80 percent of initial sales calls, the purpose is to gather information about the buyer's needs and objectives.
- Creating a favorable impression and building rapport with prospective clients are important tasks in the approach.
- During the initial contact, the salesperson strives to develop a relationship rather than just push a product.
- The salesperson may have to call on a prospect several times before the product is considered.

4. Making the Presentation

- During the sales presentation, the salesperson must attract and hold the prospect's attention, stimulate interest, and spark a desire for the product.
- Research indicates that salespersons who carefully monitor the selling situation and adapt their presentations to meet the needs of prospects are associated with effective sales performance.
- Salespeople should match their influencing tactics—such as information exchange, recommendations, threats, promises, ingratiation, and inspirational appeals—to their prospects.

5. Overcoming Objections

- An effective salesperson usually seeks out a prospect's objections so that he or she can address them.
- If they are not apparent, the salesperson cannot deal with them, and the prospect may not buy.
- One of the best ways to overcome objections is to anticipate and counter them before the prospect raises them.
- However, this approach can be risky because the salesperson may mention objections that the prospect would not have raised.
- If possible, the salesperson should handle objections as they arise. They also can be addressed at the end of the presentation.

6. Closing the Sale

- **Closing** is the stage of the selling process when the salesperson asks the prospect to buy the product.
- During the presentation, the salesperson may use a —trial close‖ by asking questions that assume that the prospect will buy the product.
- The salesperson might ask the potential customer about financial terms, desired colors or sizes, or delivery arrangements.
- One questioning approach uses broad questions (*what, how,* and *why*) to probe or gather information and focused questions (*who, when,* and *where*) to clarify and close the sale.

7. Following Up

- After a successful closing, the salesperson must follow up the sale. In the follow-up stage, the salesperson determines whether the order was delivered on time and installed properly, if installation was required.
- He or she should contact the customer to learn if any problems or questions regarding the product have arisen.
- The follow-up stage is also used to determine customers' future product needs.

Types of Salespeople

Order Getters

- To obtain orders, a salesperson informs prospects and persuades them to buy the product.
- The role of the **order getter** is to increase sales by selling to new customers and increasing sales to current customers.
- This task sometimes is called *creative selling*. It requires that salespeople recognize potential buyers' needs and give them necessary information.

Order Takers

- Salespeople take orders to perpetuate long-lasting, satisfying customer relationships.
- **Order takers** seek repeat sales. They generate the bulk of many organizations'total sales.
- One major objective is to be certain customers that have sufficient product quantities where and when needed.

Support personnel

- **Support personnel** facilitate selling but usually are not involved solely with making sales.
- They are engaged primarily in marketing industrial products, locating prospects, educating customers, building goodwill, and providing service after the sale.
- There are many kinds of sales support personnel; the three most common are missionary, trade, and technical salespeople.

Missionary salespeople

- **Missionary salespeople**, usually employed by manufacturers, assist the producer's customers in selling to their own customers.

- Missionary salespeople may call on retailers to inform and persuade them to buy the manufacturer's products.
- When they succeed, retailers purchase products from wholesalers, who are the producer's customers.
- Manufacturers of medical supplies and pharmaceuticals often use missionary salespeople, called *detail reps,* to promote their products to physicians, hospitals, and retail druggists.

Trade salespeople

- **Trade salespeople** are not strictly support personnel because they usually take orders as well. However, they direct much effort toward helping customers, especially retail stores, and promote the product.
- They are likely to restock shelves, obtain more shelf space, set up displays, provide instore demonstrations, and distribute samples to store customers.

Technical salespeople

- **Technical salespeople** give technical assistance to the organization's current customers, advising them on product characteristics and applications, system designs, and installation procedures.
- Because this job is often highly technical, the salesperson usually has formal training in one of the physical sciences or in engineering.

SALES PROMOTION

- **Sales promotion** is an activity or material, or both, that acts as a direct inducement, offering added value or incentive for the product, to resellers, salespeople, or consumers. It encompasses all promotional activities and materials other than personal selling, advertising, and public relations.
- Marketers often use sales promotion to facilitate personal selling, advertising, or both. Companies also employ advertising and personal selling to support sales promotion activities. For example, marketers frequently use advertising to promote contests, free samples, and premiums.

Nature of sales Promotion

<u>**Importance of Sales Promotion**</u>

A} Consumer Sales Promotion Methods

- **Consumer sales promotion methods** encourage or stimulate consumers to patronize specific retail stores or try particular products.
- These methods initiated by retailers often aim to attract customers to specific locations, whereas those used by manufacturers generally introduce new products or promote established brands.

1. **Coupons and Cents-Off Offers**

- **Coupons** reduce a product's price and are used to prompt customers to try new or established products, increase sales volume quickly, attract repeat purchasers, or introduce new package sizes or features. Savings may be deducted from the purchase price or offered as cash.
- With a **cents-off offer**, buyers pay a certain amount less than the regular price shown on the label or package.
- Similar to coupons, this method can serve as a strong incentive for trying new or unfamiliar products.
- Commonly used in product introductions, cents-off offers can stimulate product sales, yield short-lived sales increases, and promote products in off-seasons.

2. **Refunds and Rebates**

- With **money refunds**, consumers submit proof of purchase and are mailed a specific amount of money.
- Usually manufacturers demand multiple product purchases before consumers qualify for refunds.

- Money refunds, used primarily to promote trial use of a product, are relatively low in cost, but because they sometimes generate a low response rate, they have limited impact on sales.
- With **rebates**, the customer is sent a specified amount of money for making a single purchase.
- Rebates generally are given on more expensive products than money refunds and are used to encourage customers.

3. Frequent-User Incentives

- Do you have a —Reward Card‖ from Border's? Many firms develop incentive programs to reward customers who engage in repeat (frequent) purchases.
- As mentioned earlier, most major airlines offer frequent flier programs that reward customers who have flown a specified number of miles with free tickets for additional travel. Frequent-user incentives foster customer loyalty to a specific company or group of cooperating companies.

4. Point-of-Purchase Materials and Demonstrations

- **Point-of-purchase (P-O-P) materials** include outdoor signs, window displays, counter pieces, display racks, and self-service cartons. These items, often supplied by producers, attract attention, inform customers, and encourage retailers to carry particular products.
- **Demonstrations** are excellent attention getters. Manufacturers offer them temporarily to encourage trial use and purchase of a product or to show how a product works.
- Because labor costs can be extremely high, demonstrations are not used widely. They can be highly effective for promoting certain types of products, such as appliances, cosmetics, and cleaning supplies.

5. Free Samples and Premiums

- Marketers use **free samples** to stimulate trial of a product, increase sales volume in the early stages of a product's life cycle, and obtain desirable distribution.

- Sampling is the most expensive sales promotion method because production and distribution—at local events, by mail or door-to-door delivery, online, in stores, and on packages—entail high costs.
- **Premiums** are items offered free or at minimal cost as a bonus for purchasing a product. Like the prize in a Kelloggs Chocos, premiums are used to attract
- competitors' customers, introduce different sizes of established products, add variety to other promotional efforts, and stimulate consumer loyalty.
- Creativity is essential when using premiums; to stand out and achieve a significant number of redemptions, the premium must match both the target audience and the brand's image.

6. Consumer Games, Contests, and Sweepstakes

- In **consumer contests**, individuals compete for prizes based on analytical or creative skills.
- This method can be used to generate retail traffic and frequency of exposure to promotional messages.
- Contestants are usually more highly involved in consumer contests than in games or sweepstakes, even though total participation may be lower.
- In **consumer games**, individuals compete for prizes based primarily on chance— often by collecting game pieces such as bottle caps or a sticker on the side of
- French fries. Because collecting multiple pieces may be necessary to win or increase an individual's chances of winning, the game stimulates repeated business.
- Entrants in a **consumer sweepstakes** submit their names for inclusion in a drawing for prizes.
- Sweepstakes are employed more often than consumer contests and tend to attract a greater number of participants.

B} Trade Sales Promotion Methods

- To encourage resellers, especially retailers, to carry their products and to promote them effectively, producers use sales promotion methods.

- **Trade sales promotion methods** stimulate wholesalers and retailers to carry a producer's products and market those products more aggressively.

1. Trade Allowances

- Many manufacturers offer trade allowances to encourage resellers to carry a
- product or stock more of it.
- One such trade allowance is a **buying allowance**, which is a temporary price reduction offered to resellers for purchasing specified quantities of a product.
- A soap producer, for example, might give retailers Re.1 for each case of soap purchased. Such offers provide an incentive for resellers to handle new products, achieve temporary price reductions, or stimulate purchase of items in larger than normal quantities.
- A **buy-back allowance** is a sum of money that a producer gives to a reseller for each unit the reseller buys after an initial promotional deal is over.
- A **merchandise allowance** is a manufacturer's agreement to pay resellers certain amounts of money for providing promotional efforts such as advertising or P-O-P displays.
- This method is best suited to high-volume, high-profit, easily handled products.

2. Cooperative Advertising and Dealer Listings

- **Cooperative advertising** is an arrangement whereby a manufacturer agrees to pay a certain amount of a retailer's media costs for advertising the manufacturer's products.
- The amount allowed is usually based on the quantities purchased. As with merchandise allowances, a retailer must show proof that advertisements did appear before the manufacturer pays the agreed on portion of the advertising costs.
- **Dealer listings** are advertisements promoting a product and identifying participating retailers that sell the product.
- **Free Merchandise and Gifts** Manufacturers sometimes offer **free merchandise** to resellers that purchase a stated quantity of products. Occasionally, free merchandise is used as payment for allowances provided through other sales promotion methods.

4. Premium (Push) Money

- **Premium money** (*or* **push money**) is additional compensation to salespeople offered by the manufacturer as an incentive to push a line of goods.

- This method is appropriate when personal selling is an important part of the marketing effort; it is not effective for promoting products sold through selfservice.

5. Sales Contests

- A **sales contest** is designed to motivate distributors, retailers, and sales personnel by recognizing outstanding achievements.
- To be effective, this method must be equitable for all persons involved.

MODULE 4.3 DEVELOPING EFFECTIVE COMMUNICATION

A. IDENTIFY THE TARGET AUDIENCE

- The process must start with a clear target audience in mind: potential buyers of the company's products, current users, deciders, or influencers, and individuals, groups, particular publics, or the general public.
- The target audience is a critical influence on the communicator's decisions about what to say, how, when, where, and to whom. Though we can profile the target audience in terms of any of the market segments, it's often useful to do so in terms of usage and loyalty.
- Is the target new to the category or a current user?
- Is the target loyal to the brand, loyal to a competitor, or someone who switches between brands?
- If a brand user, is he or she a heavy or light user?

B. DETERMINE THE COMMUNICATIONS OBJECTIVES

John R. Rossiter and Larry Percy identify four possible objectives, as follows:

1. *Category Need*—Establishing a product or service category as necessary to remove or satisfy a perceived discrepancy between a current motivational state and a desired motivational state. A new-to-the-world product such as electric cars will always begin with a communications objective of establishing category need.

2. *Brand Awareness*—Fostering the consumer's ability to recognize or recall the brand within the category, in sufficient detail to make a purchase. Recognition is easier to achieve than recall—consumers asked to think of a brand of frozen entrées are more likely to recognize Stouffer's distinctive orange packages than to recall the brand. Brand recall is important outside the store; brand recognition is important inside the store. Brand awareness provides a foundation for brand equity.

3. *Brand Attitude*—Helping consumers evaluate the brand's perceived ability to meet a currently relevant need. Relevant brand needs may be negatively oriented (problem removal, problem avoidance, incomplete satisfaction, normal depletion) or positively oriented (sensory gratification, intellectual stimulation, or social approval).

4. *Brand Purchase Intention*—Moving consumers to decide to purchase the brand or take purchase-related action. Promotional offers like coupons or two-for-one deals encourage consumers to make a mental commitment to buy. But many consumers do not have an expressed category need and may not be in the market when exposed to an ad, so they are unlikely to form buy intentions.

C. DESIGN THE COMMUNICATIONS

Formulating the communications to achieve the desired response requires solving three problems: what to say (message strategy), how to say it (creative strategy), and who should say it (message source).

Message Strategy

- In determining message strategy, management searches for appeals, themes, or ideas that will tie in to the brand positioning and help establish points-of-parity or points- of difference.
- Some of these may be related directly to product or service performance (the quality, economy, or value of the brand), whereas others may relate to more extrinsic considerations (the brand as being contemporary, popular, or traditional).

Creative Strategy

Communications effectiveness depends on how a message is being expressed, as well as on its content. If a communication is ineffective, it may mean the wrong message was used, or the right one was poorly expressed. *Creative strategies* are the way marketers translate their messages into a specific communication. We can broadly classify them as either **informational** or **transformational** appeals.

Informational Appeals

- An *informational appeal* elaborates on product or service attributes or benefits. Examples in advertising are problem solution ads (Excedrin stops the toughest headache pain), product demonstration ads (Thompson Water Seal can withstand intense rain, snow, and heat), product comparison ads (DIRECTV offers better HD options than cable or other satellite operators), and testimonials from unknown or celebrity endorsers.
- Informational appeals assume strictly rational processing of the communication on the consumer's part. Logic and reason rule.

Transformational Appeals

- A *transformational appeal* elaborates on a non-product-related benefit or image. It might depict what kind of person uses a brand (VW advertised to active, youthful people with its famed —Drivers Wanted‖ campaign) or what kind of experience results from use (Pringles advertised —Once You Pop, the Fun Don't Stop‖ for years).
- Transformational appeals often attempt to stir up emotions that will motivate purchase.

Message Source

Messages delivered by attractive or popular sources can achieve higher attention and recall, which is why advertisers often use celebrities as spokespeople.

D. SELECT THE COMMUNICATIONS CHANNELS

Selecting an efficient means to carry the message becomes more difficult as channels of communication become more fragmented and cluttered. Communications channels may be personal and non-personal. Within each are many sub-channels.

Personal Communications Channels

Personal communications channels let two or more persons communicate face-to-face or personto-audience through a phone, surface mail, or e-mail. They derive their effectiveness from individualized presentation and feedback and include direct and interactive marketing, word- of mouth marketing, and personal selling.

Non-personal (Mass) Communications Channels

- Non-personal channels are communications directed to more than one person and include advertising, sales promotions, events and experiences, and public relations.
- AT&T and IBM sponsor symphony performances and art exhibits, Visa is an active sponsor of the Olympics, and Harley-Davidson sponsors annual motorcycle rallies.

Integration of Communications Channels

- Although personal communication is often more effective than mass communication, mass media might be the major means of stimulating personal communication.
- Mass communications affect personal attitudes and behavior through a two-step process.
- Ideas often flow from radio, television, and print to opinion leaders, and from these to less media-involved population groups.

E. ESTABLISH THE TOTAL MARKETING COMMUNICATIONS BUDGET

One of the most difficult marketing decisions is determining how much to spend on marketing communications. John Wanamaker, the department store magnate, once said, —I know that half of my advertising is wasted, but I don't know which half.‖

Affordable Method

Some companies set the communication budget at what they think the company can afford. The affordable method completely ignores the role of promotion as an investment and the immediate impact of promotion on sales volume. It leads to an uncertain annual budget, which makes longrange planning difficult.

Percentage-Of-Sales Method

Some companies set communication expenditures at a specified percentage of current or anticipated sales or of the sales price. Automobile companies typically budget a fixed percentage based on the planned car price. Oil companies appropriate a fraction of a cent for each gallon of gasoline sold under their own label.

Competitive-Parity Method

Some companies set their communication budget to achieve share-of-voice parity with competitors. There are two supporting arguments: that competitor' expenditures represent the collective wisdom of the industry, and that maintaining competitive parity prevents communication wars. Neither argument is valid. There are no grounds for believing competitors know better. Company reputations, resources, opportunities, and objectives differ so much that communication budgets are hardly a guide. And there is no evidence that budgets based on competitive parity discourage communication wars.

Objective-And-Task Method

The objective-and-task method calls upon marketers to develop communication budgets by defining specific objectives, determining the tasks that must be performed to achieve these objectives, and estimating the costs of performing them. The sum of these costs is the proposed communication budget.

Communication Budget Trade-Offs

A major question is how much weight marketing communications should receive in relationship to alternatives such as product improvement, lower prices, or better service. The answer depends on where the company's products are in their life cycles, whether they are commodities or highly differentiable products, whether they are routinely needed or must be —sold,‖ and other considerations.

F. DECIDING ON THE MARKETING COMMUNICATIONS MIX

- Companies must allocate the marketing communications budget over the eight major modes of communication— advertising, sales promotion, public relations and publicity, events and experiences, direct marketing, interactive marketing, word-of-mouth marketing, and the sales force.
- Within the same industry, companies can differ considerably in their media and channel choices.
- Avon concentrates its promotional funds on personal selling, whereas Revlon spends heavily on advertising.
- Electrolux spent heavily on a door-to-door sales force for years, whereas Hoover has relied more on advertising.

Characteristics of the Marketing Communications Mix

Each communication tool has its own unique characteristics and costs.

Advertising

a) **Pervasiveness**—Advertising permits the seller to repeat a message many times. It also allows the buyer to receive and compare the messages of various competitors. Largescale advertising says something positive about the seller's size, power, and success.

b) **Amplified expressiveness**—Advertising provides opportunities for dramatizing the company and its brands and products through the artful use of print, sound, and color.

c) **Control**—The advertiser can choose the aspects of the brand and product on which to focus communications.

Sales Promotion

Companies use sales promotion tools—coupons, contests, premiums, and the like—to draw a stronger and quicker buyer response, including short-run effects such as highlighting product offers and boosting sagging sales. Sales promotion tools offer three distinctive benefits:

a) **Ability to be attention-getting**—They draw attention and may lead the consumer to the product.

b) **Incentive**—They incorporate some concession, inducement, or contribution that gives value to the consumer.

c) **Invitation**—They include a distinct invitation to engage in the transaction now.

Public Relations And Publicity

Marketers tend to underuse public relations, yet a well-thought-out program coordinated with the other communications-mix elements can be extremely effective, especially if a company needs to challenge consumers' misconceptions. The appeal of public relations and publicity is based on three distinctive qualities:

a) **High credibility**—News stories and features are more authentic and credible to readers than ads.

b) **Ability to reach hard-to-find buyers**—Public relations can reach prospects who prefer to avoid mass media and targeted promotions.

c) **Dramatization**—Public relations can tell the story behind a company, brand, or product.

Events And Experiences

There are many advantages to events and experiences as long as they have the following characteristics:

a) *Relevant*—A well-chosen event or experience can be seen as highly relevant because the consumer is often personally invested in the outcome.

b) *Engaging*—Given their live, real-time quality, events and experiences are more actively engaging for consumers.

c) *Implicit*—Events are typically an indirect —soft sell.

Direct And Interactive Marketing

Direct and interactive marketing messages take many forms—over the phone, online, or in person. They share three characteristics:

a) *Customized*—The message can be prepared to appeal to the addressed individual.

b) *Up-to-date*—A message can be prepared very quickly.

c) *Interactive*—The message can be changed depending on the person's response.

Word-Of-Mouth Marketing

Word of mouth also takes many forms both online or offline. Three noteworthy characteristics are:

a) *Influential* : Because people trust others they know and respect, word of mouth can be highly influential.

b) *Personal*—Word of mouth can be a very intimate dialogue that reflects personal facts, opinions, and experiences.

c) *Timely*—Word of mouth occurs when people want it to and are most interested, and it often follows noteworthy or meaningful events or experiences.

Personal Selling

Personal selling is the most effective tool at later stages of the buying process, particularly in building up buyer preference, conviction, and action. Personal selling has three notable qualities:

a) *Personal interaction*—Personal selling creates an immediate and interactive episode between two or more persons. Each is able to observe the other's reactions.

b) *Cultivation*—Personal selling also permits all kinds of relationships to spring up, ranging from a matter-of-fact selling relationship to a deep personal friendship.

c) *Response*—The buyer is often given personal choices and encouraged to directly respond.

MODULE 4.4 DECIDING MARKETING COMMUNICATION MIX

G. FACTORS IN SETTING THE MARKETING COMMUNICATIONS MIX

Companies must consider several factors in developing their communications mix: type of product market, consumer readiness to make a purchase, and stage in the product life cycle.

Type of Product Market

- Communications-mix allocations vary between consumer and business markets.
- Consumer marketers tend to spend comparatively more on sales promotion and advertising; business marketers tend to spend comparatively more on personal selling.
- In general, personal selling is used more with complex, expensive, and risky goods and in markets with fewer and larger sellers (hence, business markets).

Buyer-Readiness Stage

- Communication tools vary in cost effectiveness at different stages of buyer readiness.
- Advertising and publicity play the most important roles in the awareness-building stage.
- Customer comprehension is primarily affected by advertising and personal selling.
- Customer conviction is influenced mostly by personal selling.
- Closing the sale is influenced mostly by personal selling and sales promotion. Reordering is also affected mostly by personal selling and sales promotion, and somewhat by reminder advertising.

Product Life-Cycle Stage

- In the introduction stage of the product life cycle, advertising, events and experiences, and publicity have the highest cost-effectiveness, followed by personal selling to gain distribution coverage and sales promotion and direct marketing to induce trial.

- In the growth stage, demand has its own momentum through word of mouth and interactive marketing. Advertising, events and experiences, and personal selling all become more important in the maturity stage.
- In the decline stage, sales promotion continues strong, other communication tools are reduced, and salespeople give the product only minimal attention.

H. MEASURING COMMUNICATION RESULTS

- After implementing the communications plan, the communications director must measure its impact. Members of the target audience are asked whether they recognize or recall the message, how many times they saw it, what points they recall, how they felt about the message, and what are their previous and current attitudes toward the product and the company.
- The communicator should also collect behavioral measures of audience response, such as how many people bought the product, liked it, and talked to others about it.

Chapter-5

	5.1 **Product Level Planning:** Preparation & evaluation of a product level marketing plan, Nature & contents of Marketing Plans- Executive Summary, Situation Analysis, Marketing Strategy, Financials, Control.
	5.2 **Marketing Evaluation & Control:** Concept, Process & types of control - Annual Plan Control, Profitability Control, Efficiency Control, Strategic Control, Marketing audit

UNIT 5 MARKETING PLANNING AND CONTROL

MODULE 5.1 PRODUCT LEVEL PLANNING

Marketing plans are developed for individual products, lines, brands, channels, or customer groups. The marketing plan is one of the most important outputs of the marketing process. The aim of planning is to shape the company's businesses and products to yield the targeted profits and growth. With a marketing plan in place, a company uses the plan to measure how effectively corporate goals have been met. `Marketing control is gathering information on marketing performance and comparing the achieved performances against planned or budgeted performances using predetermined standards and yardstick.

Meaning:

Marketing planning is the process of producing a marketing plan incorporating overall marketing objectives and the strategies and programs of action are designed to achieve those objectives.

B) Definitions :

- According to H. B. Macdonald :

"Marketing Planning is a logical sequence of activities leading to the setting of marketing objectives and formulation of plans for achieving them."

- American Marketing Association :

"Marketing planning is the work of setting up of objectives for marketing activity and of determining and scheduling the steps necessary to achieve such objectives."

Nature of Marketing Planning

- Effective Utilization of Resources
- Innovation of New Marketing Opportunities
- Objective in Nature
- Development and Evolution of Alternative Courses of Action
- Process of Grabbing the Market Opportunities
- Development of Marketing Plan and Marketing Oriented Actions

Essential Elements of Marketing Planning

1. Objectives :

Setting up of objectives is the first step of planning. It is the responsibility of the marketing executive

2. Forecasts :

Forecasting is an art of drawing conclusions about the future. Modem marketing requires a lot of accurate information, which is the basis of forecasts for future

3. Procedure :

Procedures are laid down to serve as guidelines to the actual marketing activity

4. Policies :

Policies are the guidelines for achieving the set objectives of the firm

- **Basic Policies**
- **Common Policies**
- **Departmental Policies**

5. Programme :

A special kind of planning programme helps the solution of some problems.

6. Schedule :

Schedule shows the time and period when a particular activity has to be undertaken

THE OPERATING MARKETING PLAN FORMAT

An outline of a format for a marketing plan is provided below. The marketing plan is a written document that contains four basic elements It is premised on the fact that a company must

1. determine where it is now (develop a summary of the situation analysis, including general developments, consumer analysis, competitive analysis, and opportunity analysis), decide where it wants to go (provide a set of objectives), decide how it is going to get there (provide a detailed strategy statement of how the marketing variables will be combined to achieve those objectives as well as the financial impact), and decide what feedback is needed to stay on course (suggest a set of procedures for monitoring and controlling the plan through feedback about results).

A complete marketing plan provides the specifics to all these areas.

I. SITUATION ANALYSIS

    A. Product/market analysis

    B. Customer analysis

    C. Competitive analysis

    D. Opportunity analysis

    E. Current strategy assessment

II. OBJECTIVES

    A. Sales objectives

    B. Profitability objectives

    C. Customer objectives

III. STRATEGY

    A. Overall strategy

    B. Marketing mix variables

    C. Financial impact statement

IV. MONITORING AND CONTROL

    A. Performance analysis

    B. Customer data feedback

I. SITUATION ANALYSIS

Successful marketing planning is very much a process of —if-then‖ reasoning: *If* the analysis reveals certain specific characteristics of the market, *then* our best strategy would be one selected to respond to this particular situation.

A. Product/Market Analysis

The product/market, properly defined, should contain all products or services that satisfy a set of related generic needs. The first tasks include estimating demand, determining end-user characteristics, learning about industry practices and trends, and identifying key competitors for the end-user groups being considered as possible market targets for a specific product. Some competitors may offer the same product, and others may offer a different product that will meet the same set of needs.

B. Customer Analysis

Nothing is more central to marketing than customer analysis. Customers' needs are the pivotal point around which objectives and strategies are developed. Estimates of demand, descriptive profiles, and criteria important in the purchase decision are useful in strategy design. Firms should also include market segment identification and analysis to precisely define target markets.

C. Analysis of Key Competitors

Evaluation of competitors' strategies, strengths, limitations, and plans is a key aspect of the situation analysis. Both existing and potential competitors must be identified. Two fundamental questions are answered through the competitive analysis: What is the nature of the forces that shape competition in this market? and, Which competitors are going after which market segments with what marketing strategies? The first question focuses on overall competition and the forces that influence the nature of competition in a given product/market situation.

The second question focuses on specific market segments that have been isolated through consumer analysis. After analyzing the size (potential) and the characteristics of each segment, the analysis begins to deal with competition on a segment-by-segment basis.

D. Opportunity Analysis

Opportunity analysis should identify future environmental changes that may alter market opportunities, competition, and a firm's marketing strategy. The major forces that may influence market opportunities and strategies include technological advancements, demographic and social trends, governmental and political constraints, economic conditions, and the physical environment.

To evaluate opportunities successfully, you must combine the external analysis with internal analysis, which directly influences a firm's willingness and ability to respond to opportunities. Internal factors include purpose or mission statements and company resources.

E. Current Marketing Strategy Assessment

An evaluation of the effectiveness of a firm's current marketing strategy should identify important strategy issues, strengths, and limitations. Management should evaluate the firm's strategic situation and the appropriateness of the marketing strategy being used for that situation. The process of reviewing internal operations for strengths and weaknesses and scanning the organization's external environment for opportunities is called a SWOT analysis.

II. SETTING OBJECTIVES

The basis for setting the specific objectives is the qualitative and quantitative data gathered from previous analyses. The objectives, in turn, become the basis for the development of the marketing strategy. Realistic objectives cannot be established without consideration of the operating environment and the specific consumer segments to which the marketing effort is to be targeted.

III. MARKETING STRATEGY SELECTION

After setting objectives, the next step is the development of the marketing strategy. This step involves deciding on the specific ways to combine the marketing variables to satisfy the needs of the market's targets and accomplish the objectives of the organization. In some situations, the corporate strategic plan may dictate the marketing strategy. For example, if the corporate strategy involves positioning the firm as the low-cost producer in an industry and emphasizes volume in the corporate objectives, the marketing mix would have to reflect this. The marketing mix would probably emphasize low price to generate sales volume. This would also be the major focus in promotional messages.

IV. PLAN MONITORING AND CONTROL

The final stage in preparing the marketing plan is to establish the evaluation and control procedures that will be used to track the progress of the marketing effort. Decisions should be made about the specific data needed for tracking, how and when the data are to be collected, and who is to receive what type of reports. Such data become the basis for the decisions to alter the plan and to focus on the objectives- results relationship.

Alterations in the operational plan should be made to —fine-tune‖ it or the way it is being implemented. Many companies fail to understand the importance of establishing procedures to monitor and control the planning process, a failing that leads to less than optimal performance. Control should be a natural follow through in developing a plan. No plan should be considered complete until controls are identified and the procedures for recording and transmitting information to managers are established.

Objectives of Marketing Planning

1. Scientific Assessment of Marketing Strategies and Objectives

A regular and scientific appraisal of strategies and objectives are required to be done to prove the existence of an enterprise.

2. Proper Allocation of Resources

There are three important types of resources namely material, technical and human resources

3. Identifying Untapped Opportunities

The basic objectives of marketing planning are to exploit, identify and tap marketing opportunities not only for betterment of employees, customers, shareholders but also for well being of entire society.

4. An Overall Business Growth and Development

Developing marketing strategies is a partial part of marketing planning. The past strategies insist on strength, weaknesses and mistakes committed by business while competing in time market.

Scope of Marketing Planning

Long-Term Planning :

It involves developing the basic objectives and strategy to guide future company efforts.

- Diagnosis
- Prognosis
- Objectives
- Strategy
- Tactics
- Control

Short-term or Annual Marketing Planning :

Each year companies prepare annual plan. The annual plan is developed in the context of the company's long range plan.

IMPORTANCE OF MARKETING PLANNING

- To Curtail Future Uncertainty
- Management by Objectives
- Economy in Operation
- Better Co-ordination
- An Effective Marketing Decisions
- Projective Analysis and Future Development
- Outcome of the Marketing Planning
- Better in Control
- Satisfaction of Customer
- Higher Performance Standards

Steps in Marketing Planning:

1. Scanning the Business Environment and Spotting the Broad Business Opportunities
2. Internal Scanning of the Firm
3. Setting the Market Objectives
4. Formulating the Marketing Strategy
a) Selecting the Target Market
b) Developing the Marketing Mix
5. Formulating the Detailed Functional Plans and Programmers

Product Level Planning

To carry out the responsibilities, marketing managers follow a marketing process & the product managers come up with a marketing plan for individual product lines, brands, channels or customer groups.

A) Preparation and Evaluation of a Product Level Marketing Plan:

- The marketing plan created for each product line or brand is one of the most important outputs of planning for the marketing process.

- No two companies handle marketing planning and marketing plan content exactly the same way.
- Most marketing plans cover one year and vary in length; some firms take their plans very seriously, while others use them as only a rough guide to action.

MODULE 5.2 MARKETING EVALUATION AND CONTROL

MARKETING CONTROL

In order to achieve marketing objectives as well as organisational objectives, marketing managers must effectively control marketing efforts. Marketing Control is gathering information on marketing performance and comparing the achieved performances against planned or budgeted performances using predetermined standards and yardstick. It is the process of taking steps to bring actual results & desired results closer together.

Table: Types of Control

Types of control	Prime responsibility	Purpose of Control	Approaches
Annual Plan control	Top management, Middle management	To examine whether the planned results are being achieved	• Sales analysis • Market share analysis • Expense-to-sales analysis • Financial analysis • Market-based score card analysis
Profitability control	Marketing controller	To examine where the company is making and losing money	Profitability by: Product, Territory, Customer, Segment, Trade channels, order size
Efficiency control	Line and staff management, Marketing controller	To evaluate and improve the spending efficiency and impact of marketing expenditures	Efficiency of: • Sales force • Advertising • Sales promotion • Distribution
Strategic control	Top management, Marketing auditor	To examine whether the company is pursuing its best opportunities with respect to markets, products and channels	• Marketing effectiveness rating instrument • Marketing audit • Marketing excellence review • Company ethical and social responsibility review

1. Annual-Plan Control

The purpose of annual-plan control is to ensure that the company achieves the sales, profits and other goals established in its annual plan. The heart of annual-plan control is management by objectives. Four steps are involved in annual plan control. First, management sets monthly or quarterly goals. Second, management monitors its performance in the marketplace. Third, management determines the causes of serious performance deviations.

Fourth, management takes corrective action to close the gaps between its goals and performance. This could require changing the action programmers or even changing the goals. Managers use five tools to check on plan performance, sales analysis, market share analysis, marketing expense-to-sales analysis, financial analysis, and market-based scorecard analysis.

2. Profitability control

Although sales and other annual plan analyses are critical for evaluating the effectiveness of a marketing strategy, but they give only part of the picture. A marketing strategy that successfully generates sales may also be extremely costly. To obtain a clear picture, a firm must know the marketing costs associated with a given strategy to achieve a certain sales level. Clearly, companies need to measure the profitability of their various products; territories, customer groups, trade channels, and order sizes. This information will help management determine whether any products or marketing activities should be expanded, reduced or eliminated. In general, marketing-profitability analysis indicates the relative profitability of different channels, products, territories or other marketing entities.

Marketing cost analysis is the crux of profitability analysis. It breaks down and classifies costs to determine which are associated with specific marketing activities. By comparing costs of previous marketing activities with results generated, a marketer can better allocate the firm's marketing resources in the future. Marketing cost analysis lets a company evaluate the effectiveness of an ongoing or recent marketing strategy by comparing· sales achieved and costs incurred. By pin-pointing exactly where a company is experiencing high costs, this form of analysis can help isolate profitable or unprofitable customer segments, products, and geographic areas.

3. Efficiency control

Suppose a profitability analysis reveals that the company is earning poor profits in connection with certain products, territories or markets, it becomes very important to find out whether there are some efficient ways to manage the sales force, advertising, sales promotion and distribution in connection with these poorly-performing marketing entities.

Some companies have established a marketing controller position to assist marketing personnel in improving marketing efficiency. Marketing controller performs a sophisticated financial analysis of marketing expenditure and results. Specifically, they examine adherence to profit plans, help prepare brand manager's budgets, measure the efficiency of promotions, analyse media production costs, evaluate customer and geographic profitability, and educate marketing personnel on the financial implications of marketing activities and decisions.

(A) **Sales force efficiency-** Sales managers need to monitor the following key indicators of sales force efficiency in their territory:

- Average number of sales calls per salesperson per day.
- Average sales call time per contact.
- Average revenue per sales call.
- Average cost per sales call.
- Entertainment cost per sales call.
- Percentage of orders per 100 sales calls.
- Number of new customers per period.
- Number of lost customers per period.
- Sales-force cost as a percentage of total sales, etc.

(B) **Advertising efficiency-** Many managers feel that it is almost impossible to measure what they are getting back for their advertising money. There are different models or techniques that can measure the communication as well as sales effect of advertising. Media persons feel that ids a creative field and so it should not be judged quantitatively. However, managers should try to keep track of at least the following statistics:

- Advertising cost per 1000 target buyers reached by media vehicle.
- Percentage of audience exposed to the advertisement.
- Consumer opinions on the ad content and effectiveness.
- Before-after measures of attitude toward the product.
- Number of inquiries stimulated by the ad.

(C) Sales-promotion efficiency- Sales promotion includes dozens of devices for stimulating buyer interest and product trial. To improve sales-promotion efficiency, management should record the costs and sales impact of each sales promotion. Management should watch the following statistics:

- Display costs per sales rupee.
- Percentage of coupons redeemed.
- Number of inquiries resulting from a demonstration.

(D) Distribution efficiency- Management needs to search for distribution economies. Several tools are available for improving inventory control, warehouse locations, and transportation modes. One problem that frequently arises is that distribution efficiency decline when the company experiences strong sales increases. Management needs to identify the real bottlenecks and invest in production and distribution capacity.

4. Strategic control

From time to time companies need to undertake a critical review of their overall marketing goals and effectiveness. Marketing is an area where rapid obsolescence of objectives, policies, strategies, and programmes is a constant possibility. Each company should periodically reassess its strategic approach to the marketplace. In this context, two tools are available: marketing effectiveness rating review and marketing audit. Companies can also undertake marketing excellence reviews and ethical/social responsibility reviews.

   (A) The marketing-effectiveness rating review- Marketing effectiveness is not necessarily revealed by current sales and profit performance. Good results could be due to a division's being in the right place at the right time, rather than having effective marketing management. Improvements in that division's marketing might boost results from good to excellent.

(B) **The marketing audit-** Those companies that discover marketing weaknesses through applying the marketing-effectiveness rating reviews should undertake a more thorough study known as a marketing audit. Audit is a term more commonly used in financial management to describe the process of taking stock of an organisation's financial strengths, weakness and health, through checking and analysing changes in its assets and transactions over a given period.

The philosophy of the marketing audit is very similar, in that it systematically takes stock of an organisation's marketing health.

According to McDonald, —The audit is the means by which a company can understand how it relates to the environment in which it operates. It is the means by which a company can identify its own strengths and weaknesses as they relate to external opportunities and threats. It is thus a way of helping management to select a position in that environment based on known factors. Philip Kotler defines marketing audit as, —a comprehensive, systematic, independent and periodic review and evaluation of a company's- or business unit's- marketing environment, objectives, strategies, philosophies, and activities with a view to determining problem areas and opportunities and recommending a plan of action to improve the company's marketing performance.

Meaning:

Marketing audit is systematic review and appraisal of the basic objectives and policies of marketing function and of the marketing organization methods, procedures and personal employed to implement those policies and to achieve those goals.

B) Importance :

1.Identify the Strengths and Weaknesses:

A marketing audit is a detailed and systematic analysis. It helps the senior management to identify the strengths and weaknesses of their organization.

2. Determine Problem areas and Opportunities :

Marketing audit is a comprehensive, systematic, independent and periodic examination of a company's marketing environment, objectives, strategies and activities.

3. Provide Assistance in Decision Making:

The marketing can assist the manager to understand the working of the individual parts of the organization.

Steps In Marketing Audit:

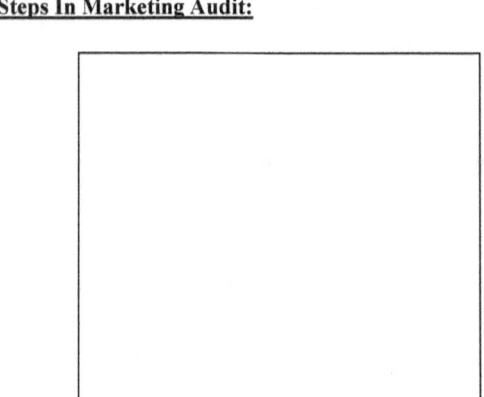

1. Setting the Objectives and Scope:

The first step calls for a meeting between the company officer(s) and a potential auditor to explore the nature of the marketing operations

2. Gathering the Data:

A detailed plan as to who is to be interviewed by whom, the questions to be asked, the time and place of contact.

3. Preparing and Presenting the Report

The presentation consists of restating the objectives, showing the main findings, and presenting the major recommendations.

Characteristics of marketing audit

Let us examine a few characteristics of marketing audit.

      a. *Comprehensive-* The marketing audit covers all the major marketing activities of a business, not just a few trouble spots.

      b. *Systematic-* The marketing audit involves an orderly sequence of diagnostic steps covering

II.   the organisation's macro and micro marketing environment, marketing objectives and strategies, marketing systems, and specific marketing activities. The diagnosis indicates the needed improvements. They are incorporated in a corrective action plan involving both short run and

III. long run steps to improve the organisation's overall marketing effectiveness.

   a. *Independent-* A marketing audit can be conducted in six ways: self audit, audit from across, audit from above, company auditing office, company task force audit, and outsider audit.

IV. Generally speaking, the best audits are likely to come from outside consultants who have the necessary objectivity, broad experience, and time and attention.

   a. *Periodic-* Typically, marketing audits are initiated only after sales have turned down, sales force morale has fallen, and other problems have occurred. Ironically, companies are thrown into a crisis partly because they fail to review their marketing operations during good times. A periodic marketing audit can benefit companies in good as well as troubled times.

Marketing audit process

The marketing audit stats with a meeting between the company officers and the marketing auditors to work out an agreement on the audit's objectives, coverage, depth, data sources, report format, and time frame. A detailed plan (who is to be interviewed, the questions to be asked, the time and place of contact, and so on) is carefully prepared so that auditing time and cost are kept to a minimum. Opinions of managers, dealers, retailers, and customers are taken in data gathering phase. After this the marketing auditor presents the main findings and recommendations. The marketing audit examines six major components of the company's marketing situation. They are:

- Marketing Environmental audit
- Marketing Strategy audit
- Marketing organization audit
- Marketing system audit
- Marketing productivity audit
- Marketing function audit

Importance of Marketing Control and Evaluation

1. Assessment of Marketing Activities:

Without monitoring and control it is impossible to assess the extent to which marketing objectives have been achieved and the strategies have been effective.

2. Helps to deal with Market Situation:

In addition, we know that markets and organizations are dynamic. The environment changes, customers change, competitors change, even the company itself can change over time

3. Promote Action:

Such systems don't just detect problems; they solve problems. Basically, actions adjust the inputs to the process.

4. Helps in Timely Correction:

It also provides the required clues for their timely correction. In a dynamic environment, marketing programs cannot be implemented effectively without continuous control and corrective adjustments

Appendix C Sample Marketing Plan C 1Copyright © Houghton Mifflin Company. All rights reserved. C 1

This sample marketing plan for a hypothetical company illustrates how the marketing planning process described in Chapter 2 might be implemented. If you are asked to create a marketing plan, this model may be a helpful guide, along with the concepts in Chapter 2.

The Environmental Analysis presents information regarding the organization's current situation with respect to the marketing environment, the current target market(s), and the firm's current marketing objectives and performance.

This section of the environmental analysis considers relevant external environmental forces such as competitive, economic, political, legal and regulatory, technological, and sociocultural forces.

The Executive Summary, one of the most frequently read components of a marketing plan, is a synopsis of the marketing plan. Although it does not provide detailed information, it does present an overview of the plan so readers can identify key issues pertaining to their roles in the planning and implementation processes. Although this is the first section in a marketing plan, it is usually written last.

Star Software, Inc.

Marketing Plan

I. EXECUTIVE SUMMARY

Star Software, Inc., is a small, family-owned corporation in the first year of a transition from first-generation to second-generation leadership. Star Software sells custom-made calendar programs and related items to about 400 businesses, which use the software mainly for promotion. Star's 18 employees face scheduling challenges, as Star's business is highly seasonal, with its greatest demand during October, November, and December. In other months, the equipment and staff are sometimes idle. A major challenge facing Star Software is how to increase profits and make better use of its resources during the off-season.

An evaluation of the company's internal strengths and weaknesses and external opportunities and threats served as the foundation for this strategic analysis and marketing plan. The plan focuses on the company's growth strategy, suggesting ways in which it can build on existing customer relationships, and on the development of new products and/or services targeted to specific customer niches. Since Star Software markets a product used primarily as a promotional tool by its clients, it currently is considered a business-to-business marketer.

II. ENVIRONMENTAL ANALYSIS

Founded as a commercial printing company, Star Software, Inc., has evolved into a marketer of high-quality, custom-made calendar software and related business-tobusiness specialty items. In the mid-1960s, Bob McLemore purchased the company and, through his full-time commitment, turned it into a very successful family-run operation. In the near future, McLemore's 37-year-old son, Jonathan, will take over as Star Software's president and allow the elder McLemore to scale back his involvement.

A. The Marketing Environment

1. *Competitive forces.* The competition in the specialty advertising industry is very strong on a local and regional basis but somewhat weak nationally. Sales figures for the industry as a whole are difficult to obtain since very little business is conducted on a national scale. The competition within the calendar industry is strong in the paper segment and weak in the software-based segment. Currently paper calendars hold a dominant market share of approximately 90 percent; however, the software- based segment is growing rapidly. The 10 percent market share held by software-based calendars is divided among many different firms. Star Software, which holds 30 percent of the software-based calendar market, is the only company that markets a software-based calendar on a national basis. As softwarebased calendars become more popular, additional competition is expected to enter the market.

2. *Economic forces.* Nationwide, many companies have reduced their overall promotion budgets as they face the need to cut expenses. However, most of these reductions have occurred in the budgets for mass media advertising (television, magazines, newspapers). While overall promotion budgets are shrinking, many companies are diverting a larger percentage of their budgets to sales promotion and specialty advertising. This trend is expected to continue as a weak, slowgrowth economy forces most companies to focus more on the "value" they receive from their promotion dollar. Specialty advertising, such as can be done with a software-based calendar, provides this value.

3. *Political forces.* There are no expected political influences or events that could affect the operations of Star Software.

4. *Legal and regulatory forces.* In recent years, more attention has been paid to "junk mail." A large percentage of specialty advertising products are distributed by mail, and some of these products are considered "junk." Although this label is attached to the type of products Star Software makes, the problem of junk mail falls on the clients of Star Software and not on the company itself. While legislation may be introduced to curb the tide of advertising delivered through the mail, the fact that more companies are diverting their promotion dollars to specialty advertising indicates that most companies do not fear the potential for increased legislation.

5. *Technological forces.* A major emerging technological trend involves personal information managers (PIMs), or personal digital assistants (PDAs). A PDA is a handheld

device, similar in size to a large calculator, that can store a wide variety of information, including personal notes, addresses, and a calendar. Some PDAs even have the ability to fax letters via microwave communication. As this trend continues, current software-based calendar products may have to be adapted to match the new technology.

6. *Sociocultural forces.* In today's society consumers have less time for work or leisure. The hallmarks of today's successful products are convenience and ease of use. In short, if the product does not save time and is not easy to use, consumers will simply ignore it. Software-based calendars fit this consumer need quite well. A software-based calendar also fits in with other societal trends: a move to a paperless society, the need to automate repetitive tasks, and the growing dependence on computers, for example.

B. Target Market(s)

By focusing on commitment to service and quality, Star Software has effectively implemented a niche differentiation strategy in a somewhat diverse marketplace. Its ability to differentiate its product has contributed to superior annual returns. Its target market consists of manufacturers or manufacturing divisions of large corporations that move their products through dealers, distributors, or brokers. Its most profitable product is a software program for a PC-based calendar, which can be tailored to meet client needs by means of artwork, logos, and text. Clients use this calendar software as a promotional tool, providing a disk to their customers as an advertising premium. The calendar software is not produced for resale. The calendar software began as an ancillary product to Star's commercial printing business. However, due to the proliferation of PCs and the growth in technology, the computer calendar soon became more profitable for Star than its wall and desktop paper calendars. This led to the sale of the commercial printing plant and equipment to employees. Star Software has maintained a long-term relationship with these former employees, who have added capabilities to reproduce computer disks and whose company serves as Star's primary supplier of finished goods. Star's staff focuses on the further development and marketing of the software.

C. Current Marketing Objectives and Performance

Star Software's sales representatives call on potential clients and, using a template demonstration disk, help them create a calendar concept. Once the sale has been finalized, Star completes the concept, including design, copywriting, and customization of the demonstration disk. Specifications are then sent to the supplier, located about a thousand miles away, where the disks are produced. Perhaps what most differentiates Star from its competitors is its high level of service. Disks can be shipped to any location the buyer specifies. Since product development and customization of this type can require significant amounts of time and effort, particularly during the product's first year, Star deliberately pursues a strategy of steady, managed growth. Star Software markets its products on a company-specific basis. It has an approximate 90 percent annual reorder rate and an average customer-reorder relationship of about eight years. The first year in dealing with a new customer is the most stressful and time consuming for Star's salespeople and product developers.

The subsequent years are faster and significantly more profitable. The company is currently debt free except for the mortgage on its facility. However, about 80 percent of its accounts receivable are billed during the last three months of the calendar year. Seasonal account billings, along with the added travel of its sales staff during the peak season, pose a special challenge to the company.

The analysis of current target markets assesses demographic, geographic, psychographic, and product usage characteristics of the target markets. It also assesses the current needs of each of the firm's target markets, anticipated changes in those needs, and how well the organization's current products are meeting those needs.

A company must set marketing objectives, measure performance against those objectives, and then take corrective action if needed.

The need for cash to fund operations in the meantime makes it necessary for the company to borrow significant amounts of money to cover the period until customer billing occurs. Star Software's marketing objectives include increases in both revenues and profits of approximately 10 percent over the previous year. Revenues should exceed $4 million, and profits are expected to reach $1.3 million.

III. SWOT ANALYSIS

A. Strengths

1. Star Software's product differentiation strategy is the result of a strong marketing orientation, commitment to high quality, and customization of products and support services.

2. There is little turnover among employees who are well compensated and liked by customers. The relatively small size of the staff promotes camaraderie with coworkers and clients, and fosters communication and quick response to clients' needs.

3. A long-term relationship with the primary supplier has resulted in shared knowledge of the product's requirements, adherence to quality standards, and a common vision throughout the development and production process.

4. The high percentage of reorder business suggests a satisfied customer base, as well as positive word-of-mouth communication, which generates some 30 percent of new business each year.

B. Weaknesses

1. The highly centralized management hierarchy (the McLemores) and lack of managerial backup may impede creativity and growth. Too few people hold too much knowledge.

2. Despite the successful, long-term relationship with the supplier, single-sourcing could make star Software vulnerable in the event of a natural disaster, strike, or dissolution of the current supplier. Contingency plans for suppliers should be considered.

3. The seasonal nature of the product line creates bottlenecks in productivity and cash flow, places excessive stress on personnel, and strains the facilities.

4. Both the product line and the client base lack diversification. Dependence on current reorder rates could breed complacency, invite competition, or create a Strengths are competitive advantages or core competencies that give the organization an advantage in meeting the needs of its customers. Weaknesses are limitations a firm has in developing or implementing a marketing strategy. false sense of customer satisfaction. The development of a product that would make the software calendar obsolete would probably put Star out of business.

5. While the small size of the staff fosters camaraderie, it also impedes growth and new-business development.
6. Star Software is reactive rather than assertive in its marketing efforts because of its heavy reliance on positive word-of-mouth communication for obtaining new business.
7. Star's current facilities are crowded. There is little room for additional employees or new equipment.

C. Opportunities

1. Advertising expenditures in the United States exceed $132 billion annually. More than $25 billion of this is spent on direct-mail advertising, and another $20 billion is spent on specialty advertising. The potential for Star Software's growth is significant in this market.
2. Technological advances have not only freed up time for Americans and brought greater efficiency but also have increased the amount of stress in their fastpaced lives. Personal computers have become commonplace, and personal information managers have gained popularity.
3. As U.S. companies look for ways to develop customer relationships rather than just close sales, reminders of this relationship could come in the form of acceptable premiums or gifts that are useful to the customer.
4. Computer-based calendars are easily distributed nationally and globally. The globalization of business creates an opportunity to establish new client relationships in foreign markets.

D. Threats

1. Reengineering, right-sizing, and outsourcing trends in management may alter traditional channel relationships with brokers, dealers, and distributors or eliminate them altogether.
2. Calendars are basically a generic product. The technology, knowledge, and equipment required to produce such an item, even a computer-based one, are minimal. The possible entry of new competitors is a significant threat.
3. Theft of trade secrets and software piracy through unauthorized copying are difficult to control. Opportunities are favorable conditions in the environment that could yield

rewards for an organization if acted on properly. Threats are conditions or barriers that may prevent the organization from reaching its objectives.

4. Specialty advertising through promotional items relies on gadgetry and ideas that are new and different. As a result, product life cycles may be quite short.

5. Single-sourcing can be detrimental or even fatal to a company if the buyer supplier relationship is damaged or if the supplying company has financial difficulty.

6. Competition from traditional paper calendars and other promotional items is strong.

E. Matching Strengths to Opportunities/

Converting Weaknesses and Threats

1. The acceptance of technological advances and the desire to control time create a potential need for a computer-based calendar.

2. Star Software has more opportunity for business growth during its peak season than it can presently handle because of resource (human and capital) constraints.

3. Star Software must modify its management hierarchy, empowering its employees through a more decentralized marketing organization.

4. Star Software should discuss future growth strategies with its supplier and develop contingency plans to deal with unforeseen events. Possible satellite facilities in other geographic locations should be explored.

5. Star Software should consider diversifying its product line to satisfy new market niches and develop nonseasonal products.

6. Star Software should consider surveying its current customers and its customers' clients to gain a better understanding of their changing needs and desires.

IV. MARKETING OBJECTIVES

Star Software, Inc., is in the business of helping other companies market their products and/or services. Besides formulating a marketing-oriented and customer focused mission statement, Star Software should establish an objective to achieve cumulative growth in net profit of at least 50 percent over the next five years. At least half of this 50 percent growth should come from new, nonmanufacturing customers and from products that are nonseasonal or that are generally delivered in the off-peak period of the calendar cycle.

During the development of a marketing plan, marketers attempt to match internal strengths to external opportunities. In addition, they try to convert internal weaknesses into strengths and external threats into opportunities.

The development of marketing objectives is based on environmental analysis, SWOT analysis, the firm's overall corporate objectives, and the organization's resources. For each objective, this section should answer the question, "What is the specific and measurable outcome and time frame for completing this objective?"

To accomplish its marketing objectives, Star Software should develop benchmarks to measure progress. Regular reviews of these objectives will provide feedback and possible corrective actions on a timely basis. The major marketing objective is to gain a better understanding of the needs and satisfaction of current customers. Since Star Software is benefiting from a 90 percent reorder rate, it must be satisfying its current customers. Star could use the knowledge of its successes with current clients to market to new customers. To capitalize on its success with current clients, benchmarks should be established to learn how Star can improve the products it now offers through knowledge of its clients' needs and specific opportunities for new product offerings. These benchmarks should be determined through marketing research and Star's marketing information system.

Another objective should be to analyze the billing cycle Star now uses to determine if there are ways to bill accounts receivable in a more evenly distributed manner throughout the year. Alternatively, repeat customers might be willing to place orders at off-peak cycles in return for discounts or added customer services.

Star Software also should create new products that can utilize its current equipment, technology, and knowledge base. It should conduct simple research and analyses of similar products or product lines with an eye toward developing specialty advertising products that are software based but not necessarily calendar related.

V. MARKETING STRATEGIES

A. Target Market(s)

Target market 1: Large manufacturers or stand-alone manufacturing divisions of large corporations with extensive broker, dealer, or distributor networks

Example: An agricultural chemical producer, such as Dow Chemical, distributes its products to numerous rural "feed and seed" dealers. Customizing calendars with Chicago Board of Trade futures or USDA agricultural report dates would be beneficial to these potential clients.

Target market 2: Nonmanufacturing, nonindustrial segments of the business-tobusiness market with extensive customer networks, such as banks, medical services, or financial planners
Example: Various sporting goods manufacturers distribute to specialty shop dealers. Calendars could be customized to the particular sport, such as golf (with PGA, Virginia Slims, or other tour dates), running (with various national marathon dates), or bowling (with national tour dates).
The marketing plan clearly specifies and describes the target market(s) toward which the organization will aim its marketing efforts. The difference between this section and the earlier section covering target markets is that the earlier section deals with present target markets, whereas this section looks at future target markets.

Target market 3: Direct consumer markets for brands with successful licensing arrangements for consumer products, such as Coca-Cola *Example:* Products with major brand recognition and fan club membership, such as Harley-Davidson motorcycles or the Bloomington Gold Corvette Association could provide additional markets for customized computer calendars. Brands with licensing agreements for consumer products could provide a market for consumer computer calendars in addition to the specialty advertising product, which would be marketed to the manufacturer/dealer.

Target market 4: Industry associations that regularly hold or sponsor trade shows, meetings, conferences, or conventions *Example:* National associations, such as the National Dairy Association or the American Marketing Association, frequently host meetings or annual conventions. Customized calendars could be developed for any of these groups.

B. Marketing Mix
1. *Products.* Star Software markets not only calendar software but also the service of specialty advertising to its clients. Star's intangible attributes are its ability to meet or exceed customer expectations consistently, its speed in responding to customers' demands, and its anticipation of

new customer needs. Intangible attributes are difficult for competitors to copy, thereby giving Star Software a competitive advantage.

2. *Price*. Star Software provides a high-quality specialty advertising product customized to its clients' needs. The value of this product and service is reflected in its premium price. Star should be sensitive to the price elasticity of its product and overall consumer demand.

3. *Distribution*. Star Software uses direct marketing. Since its product is compact, lightweight, and nonperishable, it can be shipped from a central location direct to the client via United Parcel Service, FedEx, or the U.S. Postal Service. The fact that Star can ship to multiple locations for each customer is an asset in selling its products.

4. *Promotion*. Since 90 percent of Star's customers reorder each year, the bulk of promotional expenditures should focus on new product offerings through direct-mail advertising and trade journals or specialty publications. Any remaining promotional dollars could be directed to personal selling (in the form of sales performance bonuses) of current and new products. Though the marketing mix section in this plan is abbreviated, this component should provide considerable details regarding each element of the marketing mix: product, price, distribution, and promotion.

VI. MARKETING IMPLEMENTATION

A. Marketing Organization

Because Star's current and future products require extensive customization to match clients' needs, it is necessary to organize the marketing function by customer groups. This will allow Star to focus its marketing efforts exclusively on the needs and specifications of each target customer segment. Star's marketing efforts will be organized around the following customer Groups: (1) manufacturing group; (2) nonmanufacturing, business-to-business group; (3) consumer product licensing group; and (4) industry associations group. Each group will be headed by a sales manager who will report to the marketing director (these positions must be created). Each group is responsible for the marketing of Star's products within that customer segment.

In addition, each group will have full decision-making authority. This represents a shift from the current highly centralized management hierarchy. Frontline salespeople will be empowered to make decisions that will better satisfy Star's clients. These changes in marketing organization will enable Star Software to be more creative and flexible in meeting customers' needs. Likewise, these changes will overcome the current lack of diversification in Star's product lines and client base.

Finally, this new marketing organization will give Star a better opportunity to monitor the activities of competitors.

B. Activities, Responsibility, and Timetables for Completion

All implementation activities are to begin at the start of the next fiscal year on April 1. Unless specified, all activities are the responsibility of Star Software's next president, Jonathan McLemore.

- On April 1, create four sales manager positions and the position of marketing director. The marketing director will serve as project leader of a new business analysis team, to be composed of nine employees from a variety of positions within the company.
- By April 15, assign three members of the analysis team to each of the following projects: (1) research potential new product offerings and clients, (2) analyze the current billing cycle and billing practices, and (3) design a customer survey project. The marketing director is responsible
- By June 30, the three project groups will report the results of their analyses. The full business analysis team will review all recommendations.
- By July 31, develop a marketing information system to monitor client reorder patterns and customer satisfaction.

This section of the marketing plan details how the firm will be organized—by functions, products, regions, or types of customers—to implement its marketing strategies. It also indicates where decision making authority will rest within the marketing unit.

This component of the marketing plan outlines the specific activities required to implement the marketing plan, who is responsible for performing these activities, and when these activities should be accomplished based on a specified schedule.

- By July 31, implement any changes in billing practices as recommended by the business analysis team.
- By July 31, make initial contact with new potential clients for the current product line. Each sales manager is responsible.
- By August 31, develop a plan for one new product offering along with an analysis of its potential customers. The business analysis team is responsible.
- By August 31, finalize a customer satisfaction survey for current clients. In addition, the company will contact those customers who did not reorder for the 2001 product year to discuss their concerns. The marketing director is responsible.
- By January, implement the customer satisfaction survey with a random sample of 20 percent of current clients who reordered for the 2001 product year. The marketing director is responsible.
- By February, implement a new product offering, advertising to current customers and to a sample of potential clients. The business analysis team is responsible.
- By March, analyze and report the results of all customer satisfaction surveys and evaluate the new product offering. The marketing director is responsible.
- Reestablish the objectives of the business analysis team for the next fiscal year. The marketing director is responsible.

VII. EVALUATION AND CONTROL
A. Performance Standards and Financial Controls
A comparison of the financial expenditures with the plan goals will be included in the project report. The following performance standards and financial controls are suggested:

- The total budget for the billing analysis, new-product research, and the customer survey will be equal to 60 percent of the annual promotional budget for the coming year.
- The breakdown of the budget within the project will be a 20 percent allocation to the billing cycle study, a 30 percent allocation to the customer survey and marketing information system development, and a 50 percent allocation to new-business development and new-product implementation.
- Each project team is responsible for reporting all financial expenditures, including personnel salaries and direct expenses, for their segment of the project. A standardized

reporting form will be developed and provided by the marketing director. This section details how the results of the marketing plan will be measured and evaluated. The control portion of this section includes the

- types of actions the firm can take to reduce the differences between the planned and the actual performance.
- The marketing director is responsible for adherence to the project budget and will report overages to the company president on a weekly basis. The marketing director also is responsible for any redirection of budget dollars, as required for each project of the business analysis team.
- Any new product offering will be evaluated on a quarterly basis to determine its profitability. Product development expenses will be distributed over a two-year period, by calendar quarters, and will be compared with gross income generated during the same period.

B. Monitoring Procedures

To analyze the effectiveness of Star Software's marketing plan, it is necessary to compare its actual performance with plan objectives. To facilitate this analysis, monitoring procedures should be developed for the various activities required to bring the marketing plan to fruition. These procedures include, but are not limited to, the following:

- A project management concept will be used to evaluate the implementation of the marketing plan by establishing time requirements, human resource needs, and financial or budgetary expenditures.
- A perpetual comparison of actual and planned activities will be conducted on a monthly basis for the first year and on a quarterly basis after the initial implementation phase. The business analysis team, including the marketing director, will report their comparison of actual and planned outcomes directly to the company president.
- Each project team is responsible for determining what changes must be made in procedures, product focus, or operations as a result of the studies conducted in its area.

Case Studies

Case No. 1

Sama Stores

In 2005, Sama Store not only had a great year, it also swept the top places at Punjabi Bagh, winning each of the first ten places except ninth Comfortable in the fact that the company had an attractive product, the president of Sama Store decided to go directly to the customer. The idea, instead of concentrating company efforts and resources on improving the relations with the dealers, was to emphasis improving relations with the ultimate consumer. To implement this tactic, the plan was to eliminate the dealer completely and replace him or her with agents. To say the plan did not work well is an understatement. Sama Store distributors, who ha represented it in India, initiated legal action against the Store in four states. All 323 Sama Store Audio dealers felt betrayed by the elimination of their franchises. Although they were offered the opportunity to become agents, they were so opposed that they sued Sama Store. The law suits by these dealers sought damages exceeding 50 crore. Sama Store top management decided that perhaps their original distribution system wasn't so bad after all.

Questions

Q. 1. Identify and discuss the channel alternatives that were available to Sama Stores.

Answer:

Sama Stores is obviously one of the leading producers of Audio equipments and had nearly 323 dealers all over India to distribute their products. They had an exclusive franchise to sell Sama products in their territories and as the product and service quality were good, they all had a good time until the company changed its policy of distribution.

1) The Existing Distribution Method :

According to information given in the case, all dealers were under a franchisee agreement with Sama Products. Franchise means a privilege or exceptional right granted to a person. Franchise selling is a term to describe in effect selective or exclusive distribution policies. Franchise selling in any contract under which independent retailers or wholesalers are organised to act in close co-operation with each other or with manufacturers to distribute given products or services. Franchise selling is a system under which a manufacturer grants to certain dealers the right to sell his product or service in generally defined areas, in exchange for a promise to promote and sell the product in a specific manner. The Franchiser provides equipment, the products or services for sale and also managerial services to franchisee.

Under this system, the owner of the product issues a license to independent dealers in certain areas and encourages them to make profit for themselves. The owner retains control over the technique or style with which goods and services are sold.

2) Channel Alternatives available :

When Sama Stores saw that the company's products were known and popular brands, they perhaps wanted to cut down on distribution costs and wanted to go directly to the consumers.

Therefore the company decided to eliminate dealers completely and replace them with company's agents.

The company's earlier distribution method was Manufacturer - Franchisee Dealer - Final Consumer. Now the company wanted to change it to Manufacturer - Agent - Final Consumer.

The Main Purpose of Appointing Agents :

The owners of Sama Stores thought that they could approach customers directly and establish a straight - manufacturer - customer relationship. However, they did not anticipate the reaction of their franchisee dealers.

They had all Above Options Open :

1. They could appoint wholesalers whom they would offer goods only on whole-sale basis and they could distribute directly to consumers.
2. They could appoint a chain of wholesalers and retailers to reach the consumer.

3. They could appoint sale agents through whom they would appoint wholesalers and/or retailers before reaching consumers.
4. They could appoint their own agents who would distribute to final consumers on a commission basis.
5. As the customers number in millions, direct sales through mail-order or house to house would be impractical. But they could consider factory outlets for consumers or sales through internet.

However the company chose to appoint agents on commission basis, eliminating all franchisee dealers.

Q. 2. Do you think that Sama Stores failed to properly evaluate the existing distributors? Give your reasons.

Answer:

Obviously Sama Stores did not evaluate the work of existing distributors. The company wanted the same marketing functions performed through its own agents. It must be clearly understood that marketing functions or services can be shifted or shared, but they can never be eliminated. Even if a producer takes goods directly to a consumer, channel functions cannot be eliminated. The producer under direct sale must perform all marketing functions such as buying, selling, stocking, pricing, promoting, displaying, delivering, financing and so on. The direct sale may reduce the number of times or the frequency of the functions performed, but it cannot eliminate these typical marketing functions. Further, the direct route may or may not reduce costs. In this particular case, the 323 franchisees of Sama Stores must have been doing a good job handling all intermediary marketing functions efficiently for a long time. They have invested substantial effort and time in developing the franchise and created and sustained a steadily increasing market for products of Sama Stores. True, they were free to fix their own price and could get adequate margins but they had local knowledge, knowledge of competitors, keen awareness of the customer profile, the ability to offer credit to customers, make financing arrangements were necessary and so on. The value of such experience cannot be measured in terms of money but certainly all the franchisees felt that they had earned goodwill through their efforts and would not let it go, just with a stroke of letter of cancellation of their franchise. Sama Stores, certainly failed in properly evaluating the existing distributors. What they did not recognize that by eliminating distributors, the company will have to arrange for appointment of agents, offer/space and storage space for agents, all office and accounting staff and facilities for agents, conduct daily banking operations, train sales and service personnel, arrange for logistics, treat customers according to their merits and so on.

Certainly, eliminating franchisees suddenly was a gross mistake and indicative of too low an assessment of their distributors. No wonder the dealers filed a suit of damages exceeding Rs. 50 crores.

Q. 3. Design a research methodology for conducting research for Sama Stores.

Answer:

Sama Stores, made a plan to eliminate all dealers and replace them with agents. However, they obviously did not conduct the research necessary before undertaking such a drastic step. The research must encompass all activities of existing distributors because if the company wants to undertake marketing, it should take over all their marketing functions. They should follow the following methodology before taking a final decision on distribution.

A)   Collection of Data on Activities of Distributors.

B)   **1.** Analysis of Data.

   2. Implication of data analysis while appointing own agents.

   3. Investment and return expectations on appointment of agents.

These research methodology steps could be explained as below.

A) Collection of Data on Distributors:

   i   Sama Stores could send a questionnaire to all their distributors asking for information as follows Name and Address of Franchisee.

   ii   Date of appointment and years of service as franchisee.

   iii Area covered by the franchisee.

   iv   Main products of Sama Stores sold every month - quantity and price per unit

   v   Number of salesmen, sales supervisors, after-sales service personnel, and accounts staff employed by the franchisee.

   vi   Show-room space, storage space and office space used by the franchisee-investment in space and equipment furniture etc.

   vii Transportation and packing arrangement from manufacturer to franchisee and franchisee to consumer.

   viii An approximate monetary value of goodwill earned by the franchisee through years.

   ix   The rate of growth of sale of Sama products year to year.

B) Analysis of Data, Its Implication and Investment Projection :

After getting the above questionnaires duly filled in, the management of Sama Store should try to make on estimate of :

   1) The investment, sales and profit figures for each franchisee.

   2) The amount of initial promotion, publicity and advertisement for company's agent to create the same goodwill as earned by each franchisee.

3) The manpower to be employed at each station if the franchisee is to be replaced by an agent.

4) Cost of stationing company's personnel at every station.

5) Training expenses for company's agents and salesmen.

Case No. 2

Customer Research on

Magnetic Disc Drives

Rotomatic Electronics was a small company with product line in accessories or medium to large computers. The company specialized in manufacture and sale of magnetic disc drives. The product being a complex one required extensive electric controls. As the product required high quality control it has high unit cost and was manufactured to meet customer satisfaction.

Rotomatic's business in computer industry was highly competitive. Many larger companies manufactured their own magnetic disc drives and also there were quite a large number of small manufacturers who had entered in the field recently. Rotomatics disc drives offered large capacity and high speed and could interface with any existing computers. The company could expand its operations due to attractive features and flexibility.

However, as the company was not occupying leadership position in the market, the company had to constantly come up with innovations to increase sales. In order to attain more corporate ability the management decided to diversify into new product areas. They asked the R&D department to design the single board efficient computer. As a result of six months hard efforts the R&D department created the prototype.

Questions

Q. 1. Suggest alternatives to reach the customers for the magnetic disc drives.

Answer:

Rotomatics Electronics is a small company which specialises in the manufacture of magnetic disc drives.

Many large computer companies manufacture their own disc drives and there is a large number of small manufacturers who have entered the field recently. The advantage of Rotomatics is that its disc drives offer large capacity, high speed and can interact with any existing computers. In order to attain a leading position the management decided to diversify into new product areas, so they developed a single board efficient computer. The problem before the company is to reach customers. The main strength with the company is the attractive features and flexibility of its magnetic disc drives. Rotomatics could use this strength to widen its customer base.

Various Ways of Expanding the Customer Base :

i) Internet Publicity :

Millions use the internet everyday and download large amounts of data. People also need to carry such data on their person, whenever they go and use it when the need arises. Rotomatics should create an attractive website explaining the utility of its mini size hard drives which customers can pop in their pockets or backpack to carry data wherever they go.

ii) Endorsement :

It would be a great idea to get an endorsement from a company like Zenith or HCL to say that they use Rotomatics magnetic disc drives for their reliability and flexibility.

iii) Publicity Leaflets Among IT Workers and University Students :

The publicity leaflet should highlight the low power consumption, high shock tolerance, convenience and high data storage. Emphasis should be laid on the easy to use back-up software, power savings and data security in Rotomatics drives.

iv) Publicity Posters at Computer and Accessories Shops :

A large number of people visit shops selling computers and accessories. If they see posters displaying the utility of Rotomatics disc drives, they would make enquiries and start buying the same because of their many plus points. The company could use above methods to reach a wider spectrum of customers.

Q. 2.Suggest ways and means of positioning the new product in a highly competitive market.

Answer:

Introduction :

Rotomatics asked its R and D department to design a new product and they created the prototype of a new single board efficient computers within 6 months. The company is in a situation where its main product-magnetic disc drives-is experiencing tough competition because of a large number of small manufacturers who have entered this field. The company therefore decided to go into new product areas, particularly manufacture of single board efficient computers. They have to create a market for this new product and must position the product in such a manner that it acquires a sizeable share of the market within a reasonable span of time.

Ways and Means of Positioning the New Product :

The company could use the following approach to position the new product in a highly competitive market.

Positioning Concept :

Positioning generally means identifying a market niche for a brand, product or service utilizing traditional marketing placement strategies i.e. price, promotion, distribution, packaging and competition. In case of Rotomatics, the product positioning ways and means would involve :

1. Define the Market :

Rotomatics must identify where the market is-who are the other manufacturers of single board computers, their strengths and weaknesses, prices and the market share of each competitor.

2. Define the Product Space :

Having identified the market, the company should decide the attributes or specifications of the single board computer which would be unique in the computer space in the market. Only such unique characteristics will create a position for the new product in the market.

3. Market Survey :

This will help collect information about customers' attitudes.

4. Determination of Product Space :

The company should determine the locations, the customer profiles and the price-range in which the new single board computer would sell. A marketing space therefore has to be created
in order to position the new product.

5. Marketing Strategies for Keeping the Position :

Rotomatics will have to invent newer marketing strategies in order to maintain its sustainable competitive advantage and the market position it has created for itself.

6. Symbolic Positioning :

The company has to project itself as a technology leader by carrying out an impressive product promotion programme so as to achieve symbolic positioning. These are some ways and mean to position the new product for Rotomatics.

Case No. 3
Kye - Gen Company

"Kye-Gen" is a medium size, fast growing company. It manufactures mainly the black shade. Their sales manager was impressed by sudden rise in sale of black hair dye in a rural sales area. For last ten years, the demand for black hair dye had been steady and evenly spread over the year. Sales record showed a spurt in the demand in the last year, in one quarter of the year, in that area. Same thing is happening this year also. Market intelligence has come out with surprising facts:

a. This rural area is particularly well known for the buffalo breeding and trading.

b. Sudden rise in the demand for black hair dye in a particular quarter of the year, coincides with the cattle trading season.

c. Buffalo breeders liberally apply the dye on the buffalo's skin, which then shines, looks black and attractive to the prospective buyers.

The Sales manager is happy because the overall sales figures are going up. But the marketing manger is worried, about the 'human' market reaction, if the so far little known 'animal' application becomes public knowledge.

Questions

Q. 1. What is your advice to :

a) The Sales Manager and b) The Marketing Manager.

Answer:

Background of the Case :

Kye-Gen Company a medium size, fast growing company, manufacturing quality hair dyes, mainly the black shade. For the past seven years, the growth has been steady and evenly spread over the year. Sales record showed a sudden rise in recent months and the Market Research undertaken to examine the trend revealed that :

1. This rural area is particularly well-known for the Buffalo breeding and trading.

2. Sudden rise in the demand for black hair dye in a particular quarter of the year, coincided with the cattle breeding season.

3. It was also learnt that the Buffalo owners liberally apply the dye on the buffaloes skin, which then shines, looks jet black and attractive to the prospective buyers.

Analysis of the Positions and Advice on the Position :

1) Sales Manager :

Sales Manager of the company feels happy at the turn of events as the company in any case was registering a steady growth, which only improved the performance of the company. A Sales Manager typically follows the principle of increasing sales in whatever manner possible. There will always be some reason or the other which influences or drives the sales figures and a Sales Manager just needs to be watchful and capitalise on such a occasion.

2) Marketing Manager :

Marketing Manager was also right in being concerned about the extraneous reason for sudden spurt in sales figures. It is often observed that events such as these may not have permanent impact in the long run. Many factors are instrumental in determining or in building up market demand. The possible dangers which may emerge out of the public knowledge that the dyes used on Buffalos are passed on as the hair dyes for human, has the potential of affecting not only the sales damaged. Logically speaking, the company has therefore, alternatives.

a) Temporary Sales Increase :

In Deference to the Opinion of the Sales Manager the company may take solace from the point that the sales figures are increasing over a period. However, such increase in sales is not permanent and should not relied upon in preparing the budgets and so on.

b) Short-lived Sales Increase :

Marketing Managers argument is also valid that the increase in sales may only last for a short period of the breeding season. However, from the company point of view, the company should explore if the hair dye could have an alternate use and do product research accordingly. In case such proposal becomes viable, such hair dye variant can be developed and promoted to cater to the needs of buffalo owners.

Case No. 4

The Packing Case

A certain electrode manufacturing company used to buy approximately 400,000 pcs. Packing cases in a year and the specification provided for thickness of the plank. During the annual contract suggestions were invited from the supplier with a view to economizing invited from the supplier with a view to economizing on the cost. One supplier came with the suggestion that by reducing the thickness from which was a non standard size to, the saving per case would be approximately 50 p. This was implemented with the help of the technical personnel concerned and resulted in a saving of nearly two to three lakhs of rupees per year on single item.

Questions

Q. 1. What would be the cause of thinking of a change in packing cases ?

Answer:

With rising inflation, companies would like to retain their percentage of profit by cutting down expenses and increasing sales. If the market has reached the saturation level, the only option for the company would be to reduce costs. While the main product 'electrode' is quite critical for most customers, its quality cannot be compromised. However, the company might consider saving in costs relative to administrative accounting expenses, cutting down credit periods, reducing packing and distribution costs. While appealing to the purchase department for reducing purchase costs, a suggestion came from a supplier, so as to offer packing boxes using 1/2" planks instead of 5/8" planks. This would bring down the cost by 50 p. per box. This is how the thinking came about for changing the packing cases.

Q. 2. How long might this indirect unknown loss have been carried out ?

Answer:

The company might have been using packing cases of 5/8" plank size for a number of years.The company buys 400,000 pcs. of packing cases per year. By current reckoning, it would take about 7 years for a small scale company to achieve this capacity. Thus this unknown notional indirect loss to the company must have been going on for about seven years.

Q. 3. Does it affect the :

    a. Profitability of the company.

    b. Price at which they can market the product.

    c. Marketing volume and hence volume of the turnover.

    d. Again, overall profitability to a higher value.

Answer:

a) Profitability of the Company :

Reduction in packing costs would certainly add to the profit of Rs. 2 lakhs per annum, as the saving would straight away add to the profit of the company.

b) Price of the Product :

Packing cost reduction is an internal issue and therefore, there is no reason for the company to make a reduction in the price. If the market were highly competitive, where a difference of 50p. per electrode case would bring higher sales of electrodes, things would be different. But electrodes are high-value items, and there is no need to reduce the prices because of reduced packing costs.

c) Marketing Volume and Volume of Turnover :

As the plank thickness is reduced by 1/8", the packing case, there would be some saving in transportation costs - but if the company is selling all that is produced, there is no scope for increasing the sales volume.

d) Overall Profitability to a Higher Value :

Overall profitability will go high not because of increased volume of sales but because of reduced costs of packing.

Q. 4. What is the possibility that this process is extended to other packing as well as other raw material items ?

Answer:

Certainly the management, taking a cue from this development should examine every possibility of looking at packing costs of other raw materials, and also those of finished goods too. If it is possible to save on raw materials by alternatives available because of latest inventions, it should also be considered.

Q. 5. What should be done to ensure that no such unknown loss happens in future ?

Answer:

In future, specifications of all packing materials should be checked before placing orders. Any unnecessarily heavy packing would add to the loss of the company. Similarly, all overheads in the company should be examined with a view to minimizing unwanted extra expenses.

Q. 6. How to curtail the loss to a minimum while effective action took place ?

Answer:

Until effective action takes place, all concerned departments, namely purchasing, administration and accounts should be alerted to look for all opportunities to save costs in view of mounting inflation in the market place. There should be frequent discussions and encouragement should be given to ideas which will help bring down not only packing costs but other overheads as well.

Case studies

Case No. 1

Sama Stores

In 2005, Sama Store not only had a great year, it also swept the top places at Punjabi Bagh, winning each of the first ten places except ninth Comfortable in the fact that the company had an attractive product, the president of Sama Store decided to go directly to the customer. The idea, instead of concentrating company efforts and resources on improving the relations with the

dealers, was to emphasis improving relations with the ultimate consumer. To implement this tactic, the plan was to eliminate the dealer completely and replace him or her with agents. To say the plan did not work well is an understatement. Sama Store distributors, who ha represented it in India, initiated legal action against the Store in four states. All 323 Sama Store Audio dealers felt betrayed by the elimination of their franchises. Although they were offered the opportunity to become agents, they were so opposed that they sued Sama Store. The law suits by these dealers sought damages exceeding 50 crore. Sama Store top management decided that perhaps their original distribution system wasn't so bad after all.

Questions

Q. 1. Identify and discuss the channel alternatives that were available to Sama Stores.

Answer:

Sama Stores is obviously one of the leading producers of Audio equipments and had nearly 323 dealers all over India to distribute their products. They had an exclusive franchise to sell Sama products in their territories and as the product and service quality were good, they all had a good time until the company changed its policy of distribution.

1) The Existing Distribution Method :

According to information given in the case, all dealers were under a franchisee agreement with Sama Products. Franchise means a privilege or exceptional right granted to a person. Franchise selling is a term to describe in effect selective or exclusive distribution policies. Franchise selling in any contract under which independent retailers or wholesalers are organised to act in close co-operation with each other or with manufacturers to distribute given products or services. Franchise selling is a system under which a manufacturer grants to certain dealers the right to sell his product or service in generally defined areas, in exchange for a promise to promote and sell the product in a specific manner. The Franchiser provides equipment, the products or services for sale and also managerial services to franchisee.

Under this system, the owner of the product issues a license to independent dealers in certain areas and encourages them to make profit for themselves. The owner retains control over the technique or style with which goods and services are sold.

2) Channel Alternatives available :

When Sama Stores saw that the company's products were known and popular brands, they perhaps wanted to cut down on distribution costs and wanted to go directly to the consumers.

Therefore the company decided to eliminate dealers completely and replace them with company's agents.

The company's earlier distribution method was Manufacturer - Franchisee Dealer - Final Consumer. Now the company wanted to change it to Manufacturer - Agent - Final Consumer.

The Main Purpose of Appointing Agents :

The owners of Sama Stores thought that they could approach customers directly and establish a straight - manufacturer - customer relationship. However, they did not anticipate the reaction of their franchisee dealers.

They had all Above Options Open :

6. They could appoint wholesalers whom they would offer goods only on whole-sale basis and they could distribute directly to consumers.

7. They could appoint a chain of wholesalers and retailers to reach the consumer.

8. They could appoint sale agents through whom they would appoint wholesalers and/or retailers before reaching consumers.

9. They could appoint their own agents who would distribute to final consumers on a commission basis.

10. As the customers number in millions, direct sales through mail-order or house to house would be impractical. But they could consider factory outlets for consumers or sales through internet.

However the company chose to appoint agents on commission basis, eliminating all franchisee dealers.

Q. 2. Do you think that Sama Stores failed to properly evaluate the existing distributors? Give your reasons.

Answer:

Obviously Sama Stores did not evaluate the work of existing distributors. The company wanted the same marketing functions performed through its own agents.

It must be clearly understood that marketing functions or services can be shifted or shared, but they can never be eliminated. Even if a producer takes goods directly to a consumer, channel functions cannot be eliminated. The producer under direct sale must perform all marketing functions such as buying, selling, stocking, pricing, promoting, displaying, delivering, financing and so on. The direct sale may reduce the number of times or the frequency of the functions performed, but it cannot eliminate these typical marketing functions. Further, the direct route may or may not reduce costs.

In this particular case, the 323 franchisees of Sama Stores must have been doing a good job handling all intermediary marketing functions efficiently for a long time. They have invested substantial effort and time in developing the franchise and created and sustained a steadily increasing market for products of Sama Stores. True, they were free to fix their own price and could get adequate margins but they had local knowledge, knowledge of competitors, keen awareness of the customer profile, the ability to offer credit to customers, make financing arrangements were necessary and so on.

The value of such experience cannot be measured in terms of money but certainly all the franchisees felt that they had earned goodwill through their efforts and would not let it go, just with a stroke of letter of cancellation of their franchise.Sama Stores, certainly failed in properly evaluating the existing distributors. What they did not recognize that by eliminating distributors, the company will have to arrange for appointment of agents, offer/space and storage space for agents, all office and accounting staff and facilities for agents, conduct daily banking operations, train sales and service personnel, arrange for logistics, treat customers according to their merits and so on.

Certainly, eliminating franchisees suddenly was a gross mistake and indicative of too low an assessment of their distributors. No wonder the dealers filed a suit of damages exceeding Rs. 50 crores.

Q. 3. Design a research methodology for conducting research for Sama Stores.

Answer:

Sama Stores, made a plan to eliminate all dealers and replace them with agents. However, they obviously did not conduct the research necessary before undertaking such a drastic step. The research must encompass all activities of existing distributors because if the company wants to undertake marketing, it should take over all their marketing functions. They should follow the following methodology before taking a final decision on distribution.

A)   Collection of Data on Activities of Distributors.

B)   1.   Analysis of Data.

2.   Implication of data analysis while appointing own agents.

3.   Investment and return expectations on appointment of agents.

These research methodology steps could be explained as below.

A) Collection of Data on Distributors :

x Sama Stores could send a questionnaire to all their distributors asking for information as follows Name and Address of Franchisee.

xi Date of appointment and years of service as franchisee.

xii Area covered by the franchisee.

xiii Main products of Sama Stores sold every month - quantity and price per unit

xiv Number of salesmen, sales supervisors, after-sales service personnel, and accounts staff employed by the franchisee.

xv Show-room space, storage space and office space used by the franchisee-investment in space and equipment furniture etc.

xvi Transportation and packing arrangement from manufacturer to franchisee and franchisee to consumer.

xvii   An approximate monetary value of goodwill earned by the franchisee through years.

xviii   The rate of growth of sale of Sama products year to year.

B) Analysis of Data, Its Implication and Investment Projection :

After getting the above questionnaires duly filled in, the management of Sama Store should try to make on estimate of :

6) The investment, sales and profit figures for each franchisee.

7) The amount of initial promotion, publicity and advertisement for company's agent to create the same goodwill as earned by each franchisee.

8) The manpower to be employed at each station if the franchisee is to be replaced by an agent.

9) Cost of stationing company's personnel at every station.

10) Training expenses for company's agents and salesmen.

Case No. 2

Customer Research on

Magnetic Disc Drives

Rotomatic Electronics was a small company with product line in accessories or medium to large computers. The company specialized in manufacture and sale of magnetic disc drives. The product being a complex one required extensive electric controls. As the product required high quality control it has high unit cost and was manufactured to meet customer satisfaction.

Rotomatic's business in computer industry was highly competitive. Many larger companies manufactured their own magnetic disc drives and also there were quite a large number of small manufacturers who had entered in the field recently. Rotomatics disc drives offered large capacity and high speed and could interface with any existing computers. The company could expand its operations due to attractive features and flexibility.

However, as the company was not occupying leadership position in the market, the company had to constantly come up with innovations to increase sales. In order to attain more corporate ability the management decided to diversify into new product areas. They asked the R&D department to design the single board efficient computer. As a result of six months hard efforts the R&D department created the prototype.

Questions

Q. 1. Suggest alternatives to reach the customers for the magnetic disc drives.

Answer:

Rotomatics Electronics is a small company which specialises in the manufacture of magnetic disc drives.Many large computer companies manufacture their own disc drives and there is a large number of small manufacturers who have entered the field recently. The advantage of Rotomatics is that its disc drives offer large capacity, high speed and can interact with any existing computers. In order to attain a leading position the management decided to diversify into new product areas, so they developed a single board efficient computer. The problem before the company is to reach customers. The main strength with the company is the attractive features and flexibility of its magnetic disc drives. Rotomatics could use this strength to widen its customer base.

Various Ways of Expanding the Customer Base :

i) Internet Publicity :

Millions use the internet everyday and download large amounts of data. People also need to carry such data on their person, whenever they go and use it when the need arises. Rotomatics should create an attractive website explaining the utility of its mini size hard drives which customers can pop in their pockets or backpack to carry data wherever they go.

ii) Endorsement :

It would be a great idea to get an endorsement from a company like Zenith or HCL to say that they use Rotomatics magnetic disc drives for their reliability and flexibility.

iii) Publicity Leaflets Among IT Workers and University Students :

The publicity leaflet should highlight the low power consumption, high shock tolerance, onvenience and high data storage. Emphasis should be laid on the easy to use back-up software, power savings and data security in Rotomatics drives.

iv) Publicity Posters at Computer and Accessories Shops :

A large number of people visit shops selling computers and accessories. If they see posters displaying the utility of Rotomatics disc drives, they would make enquiries and start buying the same because of their many plus points. The company could use above methods to reach a wider spectrum of customers.

Q. 2. Suggest ways and means of positioning the new product in a highly competitive market.

Answer:

Introduction :

Rotomatics asked its R and D department to design a new product and they created the prototype of a new single board efficient computers within 6 months. The company is in a situation where its main product-magnetic disc drives-is experiencing tough competition because of a large number of small manufacturers who have entered this field. The company therefore decided to go into new product areas, particularly manufacture of single board efficient computers. They have to create a market for this new product and must position the product in such a manner that it acquires a sizeable share of the market within a reasonable span of time.

Ways and Means of Positioning the New Product :

The company could use the following approach to position the new product in a highly competitive market.

Positioning Concept :

Positioning generally means identifying a market niche for a brand, product or service utilizing traditional marketing placement strategies i.e. price, promotion, distribution, packaging and competition. In case of Rotomatics, the product positioning ways and means would involve :

7. Define the Market :

Rotomatics must identify where the market is-who are the other manufacturers of single board omputers, their strengths and weaknesses, prices and the market share of each competitor.

8. Define the Product Space :

Having identified the market, the company should decide the attributes or specifications of the single board computer which would be unique in the computer space in the market. Only such unique characteristics will create a position for the new product in the market.

9. Market Survey :

This will help collect information about customers' attitudes.

10. Determination of Product Space :

The company should determine the locations, the customer profiles and the price-range in which the new single board computer would sell. A marketing space therefore has to be created in order to position the new product.

11.Marketing Strategies for Keeping the Position :

Rotomatics will have to invent newer marketing strategies in order to maintain its sustainable competitive advantage and the market position it has created for itself.

12.Symbolic Positioning :

The company has to project itself as a technology leader by carrying out an impressive product promotion programme so as to achieve symbolic positioning. These are some ways and mean to position the new product for Rotomatics.

Case No. 3

Kye - Gen Company

"Kye-Gen" is a medium size, fast growing company. It manufactures mainly the black shade. Their sales manager was impressed by sudden rise in sale of black hair dye in a rural sales area. For last ten years, the demand for black hair dye had been steady and evenly spread over the year. Sales record showed a spurt in the demand in the last year, in one quarter of the year, in that area. Same thing is happening this year also. Market intelligence has come out with surprising facts:

d. This rural area is particularly well known for the buffalo breeding and trading.

e. Sudden rise in the demand for black hair dye in a particular quarter of the year, coincides with the cattle trading season.

f. Buffalo breeders liberally apply the dye on the buffalo's skin, which then shines, looks black and attractive to the prospective buyers.

The Sales manager is happy because the overall sales figures are going up. But the marketing manger is worried, about the 'human' market reaction, if the so far little known 'animal' application becomes public knowledge.

Questions

Q. 1. What is your advice to :

a) The Sales Manager and b) The Marketing Manager.

Answer:

Background of the Case :

Kye-Gen Company a medium size, fast growing company, manufacturing quality hair dyes, mainly the black shade. For the past seven years, the growth has been steady and evenly spread over the year. Sales record showed a sudden rise in recent months and the Market Research undertaken to examine the trend revealed that :

4. This rural area is particularly well-known for the Buffalo breeding and trading.

5. Sudden rise in the demand for black hair dye in a particular quarter of the year, coincided with the cattle breeding season.

6. It was also learnt that the Buffalo owners liberally apply the dye on the buffaloes skin, which then shines, looks jet black and attractive to the prospective buyers.

Analysis of the Positions and Advice on the Position :

1) Sales Manager :

Sales Manager of the company feels happy at the turn of events as the company in any case as registering a steady growth, which only improved the performance of the company. A Sales manager typically follows the principle of increasing sales in whatever manner possible. There will always be some reason or the other which influences or drives the sales figures and a Sales Manager just needs to be watchful and capitalise on such a occasion.

2) Marketing Manager :

Marketing Manager was also right in being concerned about the extraneous reason for sudden spurt in sales figures. It is often observed that events such as these may not have permanent impact in the long run. Many factors are instrumental in determining or in building up market demand. The possible dangers which may emerge out of the public knowledge that the dyes used on Buffalos are passed on as the hair dyes for human, has the potential of affecting not only the sales damaged. Logically speaking, the company has therefore, alternatives.

a) Temporary Sales Increase :

In Deference to the Opinion of the Sales Manager the company may take solace from the point that the sales figures are increasing over a period. However, such increase in sales is not permanent and should not relied upon in preparing the budgets and so on.

b) Short-lived Sales Increase :

Marketing Managers argument is also valid that the increase in sales may only last for a short period of the breeding season. However, from the company point of view, the company should explore if the hair dye could have an alternate use and do product research accordingly. In case such proposal becomes viable, such hair dye variant can be developed and promoted to cater to the needs of buffalo owners.

Case No. 4

The Packing Case

A certain electrode manufacturing company used to buy approximately 400,000 PC's. Packing cases in a year and the specification provided for thickness of the plank. During the annual contract suggestions were invited from the supplier with a view to economizing invited from the supplier with a view to economizing on the cost.

One supplier came with the suggestion that by reducing the thickness from which was a non standard size to , the saving per case would be approximately 50 p. This was implemented with the help of the technical personnel concerned and resulted in a saving of nearly two to three lakhs of rupees per year on single item.

Questions

Q. 1. What would be the cause of thinking of a change in packing cases ?

Answer:

With rising inflation, companies would like to retain their percentage of profit by cutting down expenses and increasing sales. If the market has reached the saturation level, the only option for the company would be to reduce costs. While the main product 'electrode' is quite critical for most customers, its quality cannot be compromised. However, the company might consider saving in costs relative to administrative accounting expenses, cutting down credit periods, reducing packing and distribution costs. While appealing to the purchase department for reducing purchase costs, a suggestion came from a supplier, so as to offer packing boxes using 1/2" planks instead of 5/8" planks. This would bring down the cost by 50 p. per box. This is how the thinking came about for changing the packing cases.

Q. 2. How long might this indirect unknown loss have been carried out ?

Answer:

The company might have been using packing cases of 5/8" plank size for a number of years. The company buys 400,000 pcs. of packing cases per year. By current reckoning, it would take about 7 years for a small scale company to achieve this capacity. Thus this unknown notional indirect loss to the company must have been going on for about seven years.

Q. 3. Does it affect the :

   e. Profitability of the company.
   f. Price at which they can market the product.
   g. Marketing volume and hence volume of the turnover.
   h. Again, overall profitability to a higher value.

Answer:

a) Profitability of the Company :

Reduction in packing costs would certainly add to the profit of Rs. 2 lakhs per annum, as the saving would straight away add to the profit of the company.

b) Price of the Product :

Packing cost reduction is an internal issue and therefore, there is no reason for the company to make a reduction in the price. If the market were highly competitive, where a difference of 50p. per electrode case would bring higher sales of electrodes, things would be different. But electrodes are high-value items, and there is no need to reduce the prices because of reduced packing costs.

c) Marketing Volume and Volume of Turnover :

As the plank thickness is reduced by 1/8", the packing case, there would be some saving in transportation costs - but if the company is selling all that is produced, there is no scope for increasing the sales volume.

d) Overall Profitability to a Higher Value :

Overall profitability will go high not because of increased volume of sales but because of reduced costs of packing.

Q. 4. What is the possibility that this process is extended to other packing as well as other raw material items ?

Answer:

Certainly the management, taking a cue from this development should examine every possibility of looking at packing costs of other raw materials, and also those of finished goods too. If it is possible to save on raw materials by alternatives available because of latest inventions, it should also be considered.

Q. 5. What should be done to ensure that no such unknown loss happens in future ?

Answer:

In future, specifications of all packing materials should be checked before placing orders. Any unnecessarily heavy packing would add to the loss of the company. Similarly, all overheads in the company should be examined with a view to minimizing unwanted extra expenses.

Q. 6. How to curtail the loss to a minimum while effective action took place ?

Answer:

Until effective action takes place, all concerned departments, namely purchasing, administration and accounts should be alerted to look for all opportunities to save costs in view of mounting inflation in the market place. There should be frequent discussions and encouragement should be given to ideas which will help bring down not only packing costs but other overheads as well.

Multiple Choice Questions

Unit 1: New Product Development and Product Life Cycle

1) **The product life cycle describes the stages a new product goes through in the …..**

   a) introduction phase

   b) test market

   c) product development

   d) marketplace

Ans: d)

2) **During the introduction stage of the PLC, sales gradually increase and …….**

   a) competition becomes tough

   b) Profit is minimal

   c) more investors are needed

d) sales people are brought to push the product

Ans: b)

3) **The marketing objective for the maturity stage of the PLC is to ……..**
   a) maintain brand loyalty
   b) stress differentiation
   c) harvest
   d) deletion

Ans: a)

4) **The stage of the PLC where competitors appear is ……..**
   a) introduction
   b) decline
   c) competition is always there
   d) growth

Ans: d)

5) **Automobiles and TV's are in ……..stage of the PLC.**
   a) introduction
   b) growth
   c) post-growth
   d) maturity

Ans: d)

6) **When a company retains the product but reduces marketing support costs then it is ……… stage of the PLC.**
   a) decline
   b) maturity
   c) growth
   d) introduction

Ans: a)

7) **A company will follow one of two strategies to handle a declining product: deletion or**

   ………....

   a) modification

   b) harvesting

   c) enhancement

   d) market change

Ans: b)

8) **How long does it take to go through a PLC?**

   a) 1 day to 365 days

   b) 1 year to 5 years

   c) almost 2-3 years

   d) No set time

Ans: c)

9) **A product life cycle that rises and falls several times is an indication of ……. product type.**

   a) fads

   b) fashion goods

   c) low learning products

   d) all are the same cycle

Ans: b)

10) **A PLC curve that rises rapidly then falls quickly is indication of a ……**

   a) fashion product

   b) low learning product

   c) fad

   d) high learning product

Ans: c)

11) **The main benefit of branding to consumers is ……**

   a) they become more efficient shoppers.

   b) they have more product choices.

c) they get confused.

d) they like the new designs.

Ans: a)

12) **An organization using a name, phrase, design, symbols, or combination of these to identify its products is ....**

a) forming family units

b) trade-marking products

c) patenting product

d) branding products

Ans: d)

13) **............product life cycle stage features an emphasis on informative promotion, development of distribution channels, and low sales.**

a) Market introduction.

b) Market growth.

c) Market maturity.

d) Sales decline.

Ans: a)

14) **When purchasing consumer electronics or other high-technology products, most consumers are aware that within a year after making a purchase, it is likely that a new model or an entirely new product idea--will offer more features for the same amount of money. This phenomenon is a good example of the fact that, in general, ...**

a) product life cycles are getting longer

b) product life cycles are getting shorter

c) the product life cycle can tell a manager precisely how long the cycle will last.

d) all of the above.

Ans: b)

15) **A key difference between a fashion product and a fad product is that ....**

a) a fashion product tends to have a shorter life cycle than a fad product.

b) a fashion product appeals to a more narrowly defined target audience than a fad product.

c) a fad product tends to have a shorter life cycle than a fashion product.

d) none of the above.

Ans: b)

16) .... is the development of original products, product improvements, product modifications, and new brands through the firm's own R&D efforts.

a) Idea generation

b) Concept testing

c) Test marketing

d) New product development

Ans: d)

17) New-product development starts with ....

a) idea screening

b) idea generation

c) concept development and testing

d) marketing strategy development

Ans: b)

18) Major sources of new product ideas include ....

a) internal sources, using company R&D

b) creative approaches, using both "method and madness" approaches

c) watching and listening to customers

d) all of the above are sources of new product ideas

Ans: d)

19) The first idea reducing stage is .... , which helps spot good ideas and drop poor ones as soon as possible.

a) idea generation

b) idea screening

c) concept development and testing

d) marketing strategy development

Ans: b)

20) In the .... of new-product development, often products undergo rigorous tests to make sure that they perform safely and effectively or that consumers will find value in them.

a) business analysis stage

b) idea generation

c) concept development and testing stage

d) product development phase

Ans: d)

21) In the product concept stage of new-product development, the product is merely a

....

a) word description

b) crude mock-up

c) drawing

d) all of the above

Ans: d)

22) Introducing a new product into the market is called _____.

a) commercialization

b) test marketing

c) new product development

d) experimenting

Ans: a)

23) A review of the sales, costs and profit projections for a new product to find out hether they satisfy the company's objectives refers to which one of the following concepts

....

a) Business feasibility

b) Feasibility study

c) Business analysis

d) Product acceptance

Ans: c)

24) **Anything that can be offered to a market for attention, acquisition, use, or consumption that might satisfy a want or need is called as ……….....**

a) idea.

b) demand.

c) product.

d) service

Ans: c)

25) **Broadly defined, products include all of the following except………..**

a) money and payments.

b) services.

c) ideas.

d) persons.

Ans: d)

26) **A …………. is a form of product that consists of activities,benefits, or satisfactions offered for sale that are essentially intangible and do notresult in the ownership of anything.**

a) service

b) demand

c) need

d) physical object

Ans: a)

27) **Products purchased frequently, immediately, and with a minimum of comparison and buying effort are called …………**

a) consumer products.

b) convenience products.

c) shopping products.

d) specialty products.

Ans: b)

28) **Products that the consumer usually compares with others on price, suitability,**

quality, and style are typically called ....

a) convenience products.

b) specialty products.

c) shopping products.

d) unsought products.

Ans: c)

29) A .... is a product bought by the final consumer for personal consumption.

a) consumer product

b) industrial product

c) psychological product

d) stress-sensitive product

Ans: a)

30) Consumer goods with unique characteristics or brand identification often requiring a special purchase effort are called ....

a) custom products.

b) specialty products.

c) convenience products.

d) shopping products.

Ans: b)

31) Consumer goods that the consumer does not know about or does not normally think about buying are called ....

a) unsought products.

b) custom products

c) specialty products

d) shopping products

Ans: a)

32) The primary distinction between a consumer product and an industrial product is based on the ....

a) cost

b) size

c) description

d) purpose for which the product is bought

Ans: d)

33) .... are industrial products that aid in the buyer's production or operations, including installations and accessory equipment.

   a) Computer software goods

   b) Materials and parts

   c) Capital items

   d) Supplies and services

Ans: c)

34) Good .... contributes to a product's usefulness as well as to its looks.

   a) style

   b) design

   c) brand enhancement

   d) features

Ans: a)

35) A .... is a name, term, sign, symbol, or design, or a combination of these, that identifies the maker or seller of a product or service.

   a) product feature

   b) sponsorship

   c) brand

   d) logo

Ans: c)

36) When a brand has achieved an impressive reputation for loyalty, performance, and quality, it can be said to have ......

   a) brand endurance.

   b) brand equity.

   c) brand bonding.

d) brand prestige.

Ans: b)

37) .... **is the practice of using the established brand names of two differentcompanies on the same product.**

    a) Licensed branding

    b) National branding

    c) Store branding

    d) Co-branding

Ans: d)

38) ....is the activities of designing and producing the container or wrapper for a product.

    a) Labeling

    b) Packaging

    c) Product support services

    d) Product line decisions

Ans: b)

39) Traditionally, the primary function of the package was to ....

    a) promote the product.

    b) introduce the product to a new market.

    c) contain and protect the product.

    d) describe the product and attract attention.

Ans: c)

40) A group of products that are closely related because they function in a similar manner is called a ....

    a) product line.

    b) brand line.

    c) brand family.

    d) product position.

Ans: a)

41) One distinguishing factor between a brand name and a brand mark is that a brand name ....

a) creates customer loyalty.

b) consists of words.

c) identifies only one item in the product mix.

d) implies an organization's name.

Ans: b)

42) The following is not a benefit of multiple packaging ....

a) Facilitates special price offers

b) Increases demand

c) Increases consumer acceptance of the product

d) Provides an overall image of the firm

Ans: d)

43) Labeling is important for three reasons, including promotional, legal reasons and ....

a) Marketing

b) Branding

c) Strategic

d) Informational

Ans: d)

44) .... pass through four stages: distinctiveness, emulation, mass fashion, and decline.

a) Fashions

b) Styles

c) Fads

d) Product life cycles

Ans: a)

45) In a .... pattern of the product life cycle, sales grow rapidly when the product is first introduced and then fall to a "petrified" level.

a) cycle-recycle

b) scalloped

c) growth-slump-maturity

d) fashion

Ans: c)

46) The new product development process involves a number of stages. The best estimate of the new product's likely profitability is likely to be made at ……..

a) Idea generation

b) Idea evaluation

c) Market testing

d) Brainstorming

Ans: c)

47) To have value, a brand must offer ……….

a) A simple product range with a defined set of features

b) A complex product range with a defined set of features

c) Consistency, a reduced level of perceived risk for the buyer, and a range of functional and emotional attributes which are of value to buyers

d) An identity through which the customer can trace the party responsible for supplying the product

Ans: c)

48) An example of a convenience consumer product is ……..

a) stereo equipment.

b) petrol.

c) a motorcycle.

d) a bicycle.

Ans: b)

49) ……….. calls for testing new-product concepts with groups of target consumers.

a) Concept development

b) Concept testing

c) Idea generation

d) Idea screening

Ans: b)

50) A .... is the way consumers perceive an actual or potential product.

a) product idea

b) product concept

c) product image

d) test market

Ans: C)

51) When backed by buying power, wants become _____.

a) Social needs

b) Demands

c) Physical needs

d) Self esteem needs

e) Exchanges

Ans : B)

52) The product life cycle presents two major challenges. First, a firm must be good at developing new products to replace aging ones. Second, a firm must be good at:

a) adapting its marketing strategies in the face of changing tastes, technologies, and competition as products pass through life-cycle stages.

b) image building to ensure that products sell well.

c) primary demand forecasting so product winners can be chosen rather than making poor investments with product losers.

d) acquisition of other companies since this is the only real way to ensure new product success--go with what has worked in the past.

Ans : a)

53) Original products, product improvement, product modifications, and new brands that a firm develops through its own research and development efforts are called :

a) New Products

b) Concept Products

c) Altered Products

d) Supplemental products

Ans : a)

54) If a new product has higher quality, new features, and higher value in use than its competition , then it is called an:

a) Unique superior product

b) Synergistic Product

c) Positioned product

d) Pre –Launch Product.

Ans : a)

55) Which of the following would be a key success factor in developing new products?

a) A well – defined product concept.

b) A product priced well below market or industry standards

c) A product that appeals to the late majority

d) A product that can be sold over the internet with a minimum of explanation.

Ans : a)

56) To create successful new products, a company must understand consumers, markets and competitors and :

a) Develop a great advertising campaign.

b) Have a strong Web site to push the product.

c) Adopt a push rather than pull promotional concept

d) Develop products that deliver superior value to consumers.

Ans : d)

57) Which of the following best describes the first stage of new – product development process ?

a) Idea Screening

b) Concept Development and Testing

c) Idea Generation

d) Business Analysis

Ans : c)

58) The systematic search for new-product ideas is characteristic of which stage in the new-product development process ?

a) Idea Screening

b) Concept Development and Testing

c) Idea Generation

d) Business Analysis

Ans : c)

59) After idea generation has occurred in the new-product development process, the next stage is most likely to be :

a) Idea Generation

b) Idea Screening

c) Concept Development and Testing

d) Test Marketing

Ans : b)

60) All of the following are thought to be sources of new product ideas EXCEPT :

a) Internal Sources

b) Customers

c) Competitors

d) The local Library

Ans : d)

61) The search for new-product ideas should be systematic rather than haphazard. One way to ensure that the process is systematic is to install an :

a) Product Planning Committee

b) Venture Capital Team

c) Idea Management System

d) Delphi idea system

Ans : c)

62) _____ is screening new-product ideas in order to spot good ideas and drop poor ones as soon as possible.

a) Idea Generation

b) Concept Development and Testing

c) Idea Screening

d) Brain Storming

Ans : c)

63) One reason that idea screening is a critical stage in the new-product development process is that :

a) Product – development costs rise greatly in later stages and the company only wants those products that can succeed.

b) Competitors can quickly steal ideas so the company wants only those ideas that can be protected by patents.

c) Markets demand that all ideas be culturally sensitive.

d) None of the above

Ans : a)

64) One reason that idea screening is a critical stage in the new-product development process is that :

e) Product – development costs rise greatly in later stages and the company only wants those products that can succeed.

f) Competitors can quickly steal ideas so the company wants only those ideas that can be protected by patents.

g) Markets demand that all ideas be culturally sensitive.

h) None of the above

Ans : a)

65) A _____ is an idea for a possible product that the company can see itself offering to the market.

a) Product Idea

b) Product Image

c) Product Concept

d) Product Feature

Ans : a)

66) A _____ is a detailed version of the idea stated in meaningful consumer terms.

a) Product Idea

b) Product Image

c) Product Concept

d) Product Feature

Ans : c)

67) A _____ is the way consumers perceive an actual or potential product.

a) Product Idea

b) Product Image

c) Product Concept

d) Product Feature

Ans : b)

68) If Toyota describes one of its cars of the future as being "a moderately priced subcompact designed as a second family car to be used around town, the car is ideal for running errands and visiting friends, "then the company has just started a potential new product in terms of a :

a) Product Idea

b) Product Image

c) Product Concept

d) Product Feature

Ans : c)

69) Presenting new –product ideas to consumers in symbolic or physical ways to measure their reactions occurs during which of the following stages?

a) Idea Generation
b) Concept Testing
c) Marketing Strategy
d) Screening

Ans : b)

70) Designing an initial marketing strategy for a new product based on the product concept is called:

a) Idea Screening
b) Business Analysis
c) Product Development
d) Marketing Strategy Development

Ans : d)

71) The stage in the new-product development process in which the anticipated sales, market share, and profit goals for the first few years are described is called :

a) Idea Generation
b) Marketing Strategy Development
c) Business Analysis
d) Product Development

Ans : b)

72) When a company reviews sales, costs and profit projections for a new product to find out whether factors satisfy the company objectives, they are in which of the following new-product development stages?

a) Idea Generation
b) Marketing Strategy Development
c) Business Analysis
d) Product Development

Ans : b)

73) Looking at the sales history of similar products and surveying market opinion are tools used at which stage in the new-product development process?

a) concept development and testing

b) commercialization

c) business analysis

d) marketing strategy development

Answer: c)

74) A company is in the _____ stage of the new-product development process when the company develops the product concept into a physical product in order to assure that the product idea can be turned into a workable product.

a) product development

b) commercialization

c) marketing strategy

d) business analysis

Answer: a)

75) R&D and engineering first produce the product concept into a physical product during which of the following stages of the new-product development process?

a) concept development and testing

b) marketing strategy

c) business analysis

d) product development

Answer: d)

76) One of the unique considerations during the product development phase of the new product development process is that the _____ developed during this phase should have the required functional features and also convey the intended psychological characteristics so consumer testing can be beneficial and meaningful.

a) program

b) placebo

c) prototype

d) process

Answer: c)

77) Introducing a new product and marketing program to more realistic market settings following functional and consumer approval is carried out at which new-product development stage

a) idea generation

b) screening

c) marketing strategy

d) test marketing

Answer: d)

78) If a company wishes to test its positioning strategy, advertising, distribution, pricing, branding and packaging, and budget levels, it can do so during which of the following stages of the new-product development process?

a) commercialization

b) test marketing

c) product development

d) marketing strategy development

Answer: b)

79) Introducing the new product into the market takes place in which stage of the new product development process?

a) commercialization

b) test marketing

c) marketing strategy

d) product development

Answer: a)

80) The FIRST decision that must be reached by the company that is introducing a new product is:

a) where to introduce.

b) the distribution process.

c) the timing of the introduction.

d) the number of outlets to be included in the rollout.

Answer: c)

81) With respect to developing new products, if a company chooses to introduce its new products city-by-city and region-by-region, then the company is probably using which of the following methods for launching new products?

a) blitz

b) blanket

c) market rollout

d) market blister

Answer: c)

82) A new-product development approach in which one company department works to complete its stage of the process before passing the new product along to the next department and stage is called:

a) sequential product development.

b) retrograde product development.

c) simultaneous product development.

d) reactive product development.

Answer: a)

83) Overlapping steps in the new-product development process to save time and increase effectiveness across the various departments involved is called:

a) sequential product development.

b) retrograde product development.

c) simultaneous product development.

d) reactive product development.

Answer: c)

84) The simultaneous approach to new-product introduction does have several limitations. All of the following would be considered to be among those limitations EXCEPT:

a) it is riskier than other forms of introduction.

b) it is more costly in many instances.

c) it is too slow for many marketers.

d) it has increased organizational tension and confusion.

Answer: c)

85) The course of a product's sales and profits over its lifetime is called:

a) the sales chart.

b) the dynamic growth curve.

c) the adoption cycle.

d) the product life cycle.

Answer: d)

86) The _____ is characterized by five distinct stages: product development, introduction, growth, maturity, and decline.

a) adoption cycle

b) fashion process

c) product life cycle

d) style curve

Answer: c)

87) With respect to the product life cycle, the _____ begins when the company finds and develops a new-product idea.

a) product development stage

b) introduction stage

c) growth stage

d) maturity stage

Answer: a)

88) With respect to the product life cycle, the _____ is a period of slow sales growth as the product is introduced in the market.

a) product development stage

b) introduction stage

c) growth stage

d) maturity stage

Answer: b)

89) With respect to the product life cycle, the _____ is a period of rapid market acceptance and increasing profits.

a) product development stage

b) introduction stage

c) growth stage

d) maturity stage

Answer: c)

90) With respect to the product life cycle, the _____ is a period of slow down in sales growth because the product has achieved acceptance by most potential buyers.

a) product development stage

b) introduction stage

c) growth stage

d) maturity stage

Answer: d)

91) With respect to the product life cycle, the _____ is the period when sales fall off and profits drop.

a) decline stage

b) introduction stage

c) growth stage

d) maturity stage

Answer: a)

92) The product life cycle concept has many varied uses. The PLC can describe all of

the following EXCEPT:

a) a product class.

b) a product form.

c) a product shape.

d) a product brand.

Answer: c)

93) _____ **have the longest product life cycles.**

a) Product forms

b) Product brands

c) Product genres

d) Product classes

Answer: d)

94) **In terms of special product life cycles, a _____ is a basic and distinctive mode of expression.**

a) genre

b) style

c) fashion

d) fad

Answer: b)

95) **In the _____ of the PLC, marketers price to penetrate the market.**

a) Introduction Stage

b) Growth Stage

c) Maturity Stage

d) Product Development Stage

Answer: b)

96) **In the _____ of the PLC, marketers build product awareness among early adopters and dealers.**

a) Growth stage

b) Introduction stage

c) Maturity Stage

d) Decline

Answer: b)

97) The best example of a product towards the end of the maturity stage and or decline stages of the product life cycle is _____.

a) Cellular phones

b) High Definition Television

c) 3.5 " Floppy Disks

d) Electric Cars

Answer: c)

98) Test marketing is not needed normally under the following conditions except which one?

a) When simple extensions are introduced

b) When copies of successful competitor products are marketed.

c) When management is already confident about the new product.

d) When introducing a new product requires a big investment.

Answer: d)

99) Often in the decline stage of the PLC, management decides to reduce costs (plant and equipment, R & D, advertising and hopes sales hold up. This is an example of ____ the product.

a) Harvesting

b) Maintaining

c) Dropping

d) Ignoring

Answer: a)

100) Often management may decide to sell a product to another firm or simply liquidate it at salvage value in the _____ of the PLC.

a) Growth stage

b) Maturity Stage

c) Product Development Stage

d) Decline Stage

Answer: d)

101) The product life cycle stage, in which sales plunge to aero or drop to a low level at which they continue for many years, is the _____

a) Introduction Stage

b) Growth Stage

c) Maturity Stage

d) Decline Stage

Answer: d)

Multiple Choice Questions

Unit 2: Price

1) Common pricing mistakes include _____.

a) Determining costs and only taking traditional margins

b) failing to revise process to capitalize on market changes

c) setting price independently of the rest of the marketing mix

d) all of the listed errors

Answer (d)

2) Research has shown that consumers often use a reference process to assess what price they find acceptable. Typical reference prices include _____

a) fair prices

b) typical market prices

c) last amount paid

d) all of these

Answer (d)

3) **Market skimming makes sense under four of the following conditions but NOT when**
_____ .

   a) the high price communicates the image of a superior product.

   b) the unit costs of producing small volume are not so high that they neutralize what the traffic will stand.

   c) many buyers have a low current interest and level of demand

   d) a sufficient number of buyers have a high current demand

Answer (c)

4) **Which of the following factors does NOT lead to less price sensitivity?**

   a) When part of the cost is shared with a second party.

   b) A lack of customer knowledge of cheaper alternatives

   c) When buyers can compare prices of substitutes

   d) When the product/market offering cannot be stored

Answer (c)

5) **Which of the following is NOT a commonly adopted pricing method?**

   a) Everyday low pricing (EDLP)

   b) Cost plus and arbitrary percentage

   c) Perceived-value pricing

   d) Target-return pricing

Answer (b)

6) **Other pricing methods include four of the following but NOT** _____ .

   a) open-bids\

b) English auctions (ascending bids)

c) dutch auctions (descending bids)

d) auction-type pricing

Answer (c)

7) **Which of the following is NOT normally recognised as a leading form of price discounting?**

   a) Functional discount

   b) Quantity discount

   c) Cash discount

   d) Personal discount

Answer (d)

8) **A price cutting strategy can lead to _____ .**

   a) low-quality trap

   b) shallow-pockets trap

   c) price-war trap

   d) all of these traps

Answer (d)

9) **There are a number of factors that need to be taken into account when pricing products and services globally which can be generally categorized into:**

   a) Firm level, product specific, channel specific and retailer type.

   b) Firm level, product specific, market specific and environmental.

   c) Brand image, channel specific and environmental.

   d) Brand positioning, product specific, market specific and environment.

Answer (b)

10) **The minimum selling price that a firm can sustain for a product is determined by:**

   a) What it costs to produce.

   b) Competitors prices.

   c) What customers are prepared to pay for it.

d) Competitive parity.

Answer (d)

11) Price discrimination by a firm implies that it:

  a) Matches selling prices closely to production costs.

  b) Charges some groups more than others.

  c) Minimizes its costs.

  d) Publishes price lists.

Answer(b)

12) A company entering a new market with low initial prices is most likely to be influenced in the short-term by which type of objectives?

  a) Social objectives

  b) Personal objectives

  c) Market share objectives

  d) Profit maximization objectives

Answer (c)

13) A_____ strategy offers the flexibility which allows organizations to charge differential prices, according to market conditions, and may offer the best long term pricing solution.

  a) Corridor pricing

  b) Standardization

  c) Adaptation

  d) Poly centric

 Answer (a)

14) Price escalation is:

a) Carrying out price increases.

b) Changes in price due to inflation.

c) Additions to the basic selling price due to all intermediates adding a margin for services.

d) Additions to the basic selling price because retailers and wholesalers add their margins.

Answer (c)

15) Transfer pricing is due to:

a) The operations of parallel or 'grey' marketers.

b) Counter trading by countries.

c) A way for International marketers to avoid paying tax.

d) International marketers transferring goods and services in their organization between different countries.

Answer (d)

16) A fixed-price policy is one where:

a) Different prices are charged to buyers based on the individual customers and situations. **b)** Price fixing is allowed by the government.

c) Setting one price for all buyers is the norm.

d) Different prices are charged based on barter or negotiation.

Answer (c)

17) All of the following would be considered to be among the internal factors that affect price decisions EXCEPT:

a) Marketing objectives.

b) Organizational considerations.

c) Costs.

d) Competition.

Answer (d)

18) All of the following would be considered to be among the external factors that affect price decisions EXCEPT:

a) Costs.

b) Nature of the market and demand.

c) Environmental factors such as the economy and social concerns.

d) Competition.

Answer (a)

19) Common price objectives include the following: (Select the best set)

a) Current profit maximization and promotional push strategies.

b) Predatory pricing and soft sell strategies.

c) Product quality leadership and promotional pull strategies.

d) Current profit maximization and market share leadership.

Answer (d)

20) Most firms want to avoid pricing that turns their products into:

a) Commodities

b) Service goods.

c) Shopping goods.

d) Specialty goods.

Answer (a)

21) According to the text, _____ is a variation of target profit pricing.

a) break-even pricing

b) buyer-based pricing

c) going-rate pricing

d) competition-based pricing

Answer (a)

22) **If price is used to say something about the product other than in just economic terms, a pricing method is being used called:**

a) Promotional pricing.

b) Psychological pricing.

c) Discount and allowance pricing.

d) Segmented pricing.

Answer (b)

23) **_____ implies that the prices in the individual countries may only vary within a set range.**

a) A price corridor

b) Barter

c) Standardized pricing

d) Transfer pricing

Answer (a)

24) **_____ is a company's power to maintain or even raise prices without losing market share.**

a) Target cost

b) Variable cost

c) Unit cost

d) Pricing power

Answer (d)

25) **_____ pricing is product driven. The company designs what it considers to be a good product, totals the expenses of making the product, and sets a price that covers costs plus a target profit.**

a) Value-based

b) Skimming

c) Cost-based

d) Variable

Answer (c)

26) Under _____, the market consists of a few sellers who are highly sensitive to each other's pricing and marketing strategies.

a) monopolistic competition

b)pure competition

c) oligopolistic competition

d) a pure monopoly

Answer (b)

27) If demand hardly changes with a small change in price, we say the demand is _____.

   a) Variable

   b) Inelastic

   c) at break-even pricing

   d) value-based

Answer (b)

28) When companies set prices, the government and social concerns are two _____ affecting pricing decisions.

a) external factors

b) demand curves

c)economic conditions

d) temporary influences

Answer (a)

29) **Which of the following is NOT an objective of discounts?**

   a) Reward valuable customers

   b) Reward Competitors

   c) Move out of date stock

   d) Increase short term sales

Answer (b)

30) **Aggressive pricing is associated with which of the following stage of product life cycle?**

   a) Introduction

   b) Growth

   c) Maturity

   d) Decline

Answer (c)

31) **Which of the following is a pricing technique used by retailers?**

   a) Cost push pricing

   b) Cost –plus pricing

   c) Demand –pull pricing

   d) Demand push pricing

Answer (b)

32) **A company wants prompt payment from the customers. What type of discount will be suitable for the company?**

   a) Seasonal discount

   b) Trade discount

   c) Quantity Discount

   d) Cash Discount

Answer (d)

33) **What is price skimming?**

a) Setting a low price to "skim off" a large number of consumers.

b) Setting an initially – high price which falls as competitors enter the market.

c) Setting a high price which consumers perceive as indicating high quality

d) Setting price based on competitors pricing

Answer (b)

34) Setting a price below that of the competition is called:

   a) Skimming

   b) Competitive pricing

   c) Penetration pricing

   d) Cost plus pricing

Answer (c)

35) A change in total cost caused by adding one or more unit to the production total is called

   a) Variable cost

   b) Marginal cost

   c) Fixed cost

   d) Basic cost

Answer (b)

36) A cost which does not vary no matter how much is produced is called

   a) Marginal cost

   b) Fixed cost

   c) Basic cost

   d) Total cost

Answer (b)

37) Calculating prices on the basis of what the market will pay is called

   a) Competitive pricing

   b) Prestige pricing

   c) Demand pricing

   d) Skimming pricing

Answer (c)

38) **Ending prices with 99p is called**

   a) Odd –even pricing

   b) Price lining

   c) Prestige pricing

   d) Skimming pricing

Answer (a)

39) **Bundle pricing is**

   a) Packaging a group of products together

   b) Providing a bundle of benefits for one price

   c) Providing a group of prices for one product category

   d) Packaging a product and giving a price to it

Answer (a)

40) **Which of the following is <u>not</u> a reason for a company to initiate a price cut?**

   a) to obtain prestige

   b) to dominate the market

   c) to boost sales

   d) to influence falling demand

Answer (a)

41) **If price is used to say something about the product other than in just economic term, a pricing method is being used called:**

   a) Segmented pricing

   b) Psychological pricing

   c) Promotional pricing

   d) Discount and allowance pricing

Answer (b)

42) **Theatres and sports teams often sell season tickets at less than the cost of a single ticket to promote long-term sales. This form of pricing is most appropriately called:**

a) By product pricing

b) Psychological pricing

c) Product – bundle pricing

d) Sealed – bid pricing

Answer (c)

43) **Market-skimming pricing would likely be most effective in selling _____.**

a) anything easily copied by competitors.

b) an electronic device for which research and development must be recouped

c) most items at EDLP retailers such as Wal-Mart

d) any convenience item

Answer (b)

44) **Throughout most of history, prices were set by _____.**

a) Fixed-price policies constructed by sellers

b) Negotiation between buyers and sellers

c) Governments and regulatory agencies

d) Ruling monarchs

Answer: (b)

45) **Theatres and sports teams often sell season tickets at less than the cost of a single ticket to promote long-term sales. This form of pricing is most appropriately called:**

a) By product pricing

b) Psychological pricing

c) Product – bundle pricing

d) Sealed – bid pricing

Answer: (c)

46) **In marketing terms, _____ refers to what we get for what we pay:**

a) Revenue

b) Cost

c) Value

d) Product

Answer: (c)

47) _____ act as cues by indicating to a potential customer that there is a bargain to be had.

a) Odd number pricing

b) Sale signs

c) Relative price

d) Price surplus

Answer: (b)

48) _____vary according to the number of units of goods made or services sold.

a) Product assets

b) Price elasticity

c) Fixed costs

d) Variable costs

Answer:(d)

49) **The two dominant approaches to pricing new propositions are:**

a) negotiated pricing and discount pricing method

b) transfer pricing and relationship pricing method

c) the market skimming pricing and the market penetration pricing method.

d) value-in-use pricing and transfer pricing method

Answer: (c)

50) _____ **is the amount of money charged for a product or service.**

a) Price

b) Accountancy

c) Demand

d) Value

Answer: (a)

51) _____ is the sum of the values that consumers exchange for the benefits of having or using the product or service.

a) Price

b) Elasticity

c) Demand

d) Value estimate

Answer: (a)

52) Throughout most of history, prices were set by _____.

a) fixed-price policies constructed by sellers

b) negotiation between buyers and sellers

c) governments and regulatory agencies

d) ruling monarchs

Answer: (b)

53) A _____ policy means that a firm sets one price for all buyers in a given product or service line.

a) fixed-price

b) variable-price

c) dynamic-price

d) standard-price

Answer: (a)

54) Which of the following factors is spurring a new movement in pricing toward dynamic pricing?

a) the federal government

b) strong retailers

c) the Internet

d) strong wholesalers

Answer: (b)

55) _____ **is the practice of charging different prices depending on individual**

customers and situations.

a) Fixed-pricing

b) Standard-pricing

c) Barter-pricing

d) Dynamic pricing

Answer: (d)

56) _____ is the only element of the marketing mix that produces revenue.

a) Product

b) Price

c) Place (distribution)

d) Promotion

Answer: (b)

57) Before setting price, the company must decide on its strategy for:

a) distribution.

b) promotion.

c) the environment.

d) the product.

Answer: (d)

58) Companies set _____ as their major objective if they are troubled by too   much
capacity, heavy competition, or changing consumer wants.

a) current profit maximization

b) survival

c) market share leadership

d) product quality leadership

Answer: (b)

59) **Pricing to cover variable costs and some fixed costs, as in the case of some automobile distributorships that sell below total costs, is typical of which of the following pricing objectives?**

a) current profit maximization

b) product quality leadership

c) market share leadership

d) survival

Answer: (d)

60) Choosing a price based upon its short-term effect on current profit, cash flow, or return on investment reflects which of the following pricing objectives?

a) current profit maximization

b) product quality leadership

c) market share leadership

d) survival

Answer: (a)

61) If a company believes that the company with the largest market share will enjoy the lowest costs and highest long-run profits, that company will probably choose which of the following pricing objectives as their primary course of action?

a) current profit maximization

b) product quality leadership

c) market share leadership

d) survival

Answer: (c)

62) When a company sets a price for a new product on the basis of what it thinks the product should cost, then develops estimates on what each component should cost to meet the proposed price with an acceptable profit margin, the company is practicing:

a) predatory pricing.
b) target costing.
c) strategic pricing.
d) low cost leadership.

Answer: (b)

63) _____ set(s) the floor for the price that the company can charge for its product.

a) Supply
b) Demand
c) Costs
d) Nonprofit factors

Answer: (c)

64) Companies with _____ can set lower prices that result in greater sales and profits.

a) lower market share percentages
b) higher costs
c) lower costs
d) larger supply ratios

Answer: (c)

65) Costs that do not vary with production or sales levels are called:

a) fixed costs.
b) variable costs.
c) standard costs.
d) independent costs.

Answer: (a) Difficulty: (1) Page: 359

66) In industries such as aerospace, steel, railroads, and oil, companies often have a
_____ to set the prices or to help others in setting them.
   a) Vice-President of Pricing
   b) Pricing Board
   c) Pricing Department
   d) PFO (Pricing and Financial Officer)

Answer: (c)

67) Non regulated monopolies are free to price at what the market will bear. However,
they do not always charge the full price for a number of reasons. One of those reasons
is the:
   a) desire to skim profits is usually low.
   b) desire to penetrate the market faster with a low price.
   c) fear of global cultural reaction.
   d) damage that high pricing does to corporate culture.

Answer: (b)

68) The _____ is a curve that shows the number of units the market will buy in a
given time period, at different prices that might be charged.
   a) price curve
   b) cost curve
   c) supply curve
   d) demand curve

Answer: (d)

69) With respect to the demand curve (in the normal case), demand and price are:
   a) directly related.
   b) parallel.
   c) inversely related.
   d) related only through "the invisible hand" of the market place.

Answer: (c)

70) _____ is a measure of the sensitivity of demand to changes in price.

a) Price sensitivity

b) Price comparability

c) Price elasticity

d) Price response

Answer: (c)

71) If the demand hardly changes with a small change in price, we can say that the demand is classified as being:

a) neutral.

b) elastic.

c) kinked.

d) inelastic.

Answer: (d)

72) If demand is elastic rather than inelastic, sellers will consider:

a) lowering their price.

b) raising their price.

c) acquiring competitors as a means of avoiding price competition.

d) maintaining the status quo.

Answer: (a)

73) All of the following are considered to be forms of a cost-based approach to pricing EXCEPT:

a) cost-plus pricing.

b) break-even analysis.

c) going-rate pricing.

d) target profit pricing.

Answer: (c)

74) Adding a standard markup to the cost of the product refers to:

a) cost-plus pricing.

b) break-even analysis.

c) target profit pricing.

d) perceived-value pricing.

Answer: (a)

75) Markup pricing remains popular in the marketplace. Which of the following is a reason for this popularity?
   a) Cost-plus pricing favors the best price.
   b) Standard markups make the most sense.
   c) Cost-plus pricing is fairer to both buyers and sellers.
   d) The method focuses on demand as its base.

Answer: (c)

76) Setting prices to break even on the costs of making and marketing a product or make the target profit it is seeking is called:
   a) cost-plus pricing.
   b) perceived-value pricing.
   c) break-even pricing.
   d) Going-rate pricing.

Answer: (c)

77) **Which of the following would be considered to be one of the major faults of break-even analysis and target profit pricing?**
   a) They do not take into account the price-demand relationship.
   b) They are very complicated to calculate.
   c) There are serious time lags in the calculations.
   d) Most managers do not have confidence in the methods.

Answer: (a)

78) The pricing method that uses the buyer's point of view regarding the worth of a product, not the seller's cost, is called:
   a) cost-plus pricing.
   b) value-based pricing.
   c) break-even pricing.
   d) going-rate pricing.

Answer: (b)

79) When a coffee shop in an airport and a fine restaurant in a luxury hotel charge different prices for the same meal to customers who find the atmosphere in the hotel worth the difference in price, we can say that _____ was being used.

a) value-based pricing
b) cost-plus pricing
c) break-even pricing
d) going-rate pricing

Answer: (a)

80) Which of the following pricing methods uses the idea that pricing begins with analyzing consumer needs and value perceptions, and price is set to match consumer's perceived value?

a) cost-based pricing
b) service-based pricing
c) psychology-based pricing
d) value-based pricing

Answer: (d)

81) _____ is offering just the right combination of quality and good service at a fair price.

a) Value pricing
b) Cost pricing
c) Service pricing
d) Demand pricing

Answer: (a)

82) _____ pricing involves charging higher prices on an everyday basis but running frequent promotions to lower prices temporarily on selected items below the EDLP (Every day Low Price) level.

a) Fair
b) Low-high

c) High-low

d) Promotional

Answer: (c)

83) If the customers base their judgments of a product's value on the prices that competitors charge for similar products, then _____ is in place.

a) cost-plus pricing

b) value-based pricing

c) competition-based pricing

d) target profit pricing

Answer: (c)

84) When demand elasticity is hard to measure, and firms tend to price according to the "collective wisdom" of the industry, the pricing method most likely to be used is called:

a) cost-plus pricing.

b) break-even pricing.

c) sealed-bid pricing.

d) going-rate pricing.

Answer: (d)

85) Companies bringing out a new product face the challenge of setting prices for the first time. They can choose between two broad strategies. What are these two broad strategies?

a) product mix strategies and pricing mix strategies

b) product line pricing and captive-product pricing

c) market-skimming pricing and market-penetration pricing

d) market-expansion pricing and market-harvesting pricing

Answer: (c)

86) The process of setting a high price for a new product to gain maximum revenues layer by layer from the segments willing to pay the high price is called:

a) Market - penetration pricing.

b) Market – layer pricing.

c) Market - skimming pricing.

d) Market - saturation pricing.

Answer: (c)

87) Market skimming makes sense only under certain conditions. Which of the following WOULD NOT be a reason for using market skimming pricing?

a) The market must be highly price sensitive.

b) The product's quality and image must support its higher price, and enough buyers must want the product at that price.

c) The costs of producing a smaller volume cannot be so high that they cancel the dvantage of charging more.

d) Competitors should not be able to enter the market easily and undercut the high price.

Answer: (a)

88) Setting a low initial price to attract a large number of buyers quickly and win a large market share is called:

a) market-penetration pricing.

b) market-skimming pricing.

c) market-loss pricing.

d) market-competitive pricing.

Answer: (a)

89) Market-penetration pricing refers to the practice of:

a) setting a high initial price and then penetrating the market with successive prices for each price sensitive layer.

b) setting a low initial price to penetrate the market quickly and attract a large number of buyers to win a large market share.

c) pricing to attract low volume in many segments so as to gradually penetrate the market as a whole.

d) pricing products very high to penetrate deeply and quickly into large profits for the company.

Answer: (b)

90) When Dell Computer runs an advertisement that boosts "Superior Quality, Superior Service, and Unbelievable Price," they are most likely using which of the following new product pricing strategies?
   a) market-penetration pricing
   b) market-skimming pricing
   c) market-loss pricing
   d) market-competitive pricing

Answer: (a)

91) _____ is setting the price steps between various products in a product line based on cost differences between the products, customer evaluations of different features, and competitors' prices.
   a) Optional-product pricing
   b) captive-product pricing
   c) product line pricing
   d) by-product pricing

Answer: (c)

92) The use of price points for reference to different levels of quality for a company's related products is typical of which product-mix pricing strategy?
   a) optional-product pricing
   b) captive-product pricing
   c) by-product pricing
   d) product line pricing

Answer: (d) Difficulty: (2) Page: 373

93) Using a low sticker price on automobiles to attract customers and then selling models with additional accessory features to meet customer needs is a form of which of the following pricing strategies?
   a) optional-product pricing
   b) captive-product pricing

c) by-product pricing

d) product line pricing

Answer: (a)

94) _____ is setting a price for products that must be used along with a main

product, such as blades for a razor.

a) Optional-product pricing

b) Captive-product pricing

c) By-product pricing

d) Product line pricing

Answer: (b)

95) Captive-product pricing applies to services pricing. With respect to services, the captive-
product strategy is called :

a) demand pricing.

b) slack pricing.

c) two-part pricing.

d) referral pricing.

Answer: (c)

96) **_____ is setting a price for by-products in order to make the main**

product's price more competitive.

a) Optional-product pricing

b) Captive-product pricing

c) By-product pricing

d) Product line pricing

Answer: (c)

97) **Combining several products and offering them together at a reduced price is called:**

a) product-bundle pricing.

b) optional-product pricing.

c) captive-product pricing.

d) by-product pricing.

Answer: (a)

98) All of the following are price-adjustment strategies EXCEPT:

a) segmented pricing.

b) market-penetration pricing.

c) psychological pricing.

d) promotional pricing.

Answer: (b)

99) A price reduction to buyers who buy in large volumes is called a:

a) quantity discount.

b) cash discount.

c) seasonal discount.

d) trade discount.

Answer: (a)

100) A(n) _____ is a straight reduction in price on purchases during a stated period of time.

a) allowance

b) discount

c) pricing segment

d) reference price

Answer: (b)

101) **A(n) _____ is a price reduction to buyers who pay their bills promptly.**

a) quantity discount

b) functional discount

c) cash discount

d) allowance

Answer: (c)

102) **In an attempt to keep production steady during an entire year, especially for products whose use is for only part of the year, sellers often use which of the following?**

a) cash discounts

b) quantity discounts

c) functional discounts

d) seasonal discounts

Answer: (d)

103) A functional discount is also called a _____ discount.

a) segmented

b) quantity

c) trade

d) service

Answer: (c)

104) Promotional money paid by manufacturers to retailers in return for an agreement to feature the manufacturer's products in some way is called a(n):

a) discount.

b) allowance.

c) rebate.

d) off-retail price.

Answer: (b)

105) If a state university charges different tuition rates to in-state and out-of-state students, then the university is practicing a form of:

a) promotional pricing.

b) institutional pricing.

c) segmented pricing.

d) psychological pricing.

Answer: (c)

106) When different versions of a product are priced differently but not in accordance to differences in their value, it is a form of:

a) customer-segment pricing.

b) product-form pricing.

c) location pricing.

d) time pricing.

Answer: (b)

107) **Prices that buyers carry in their minds and refer to when they look at a given product   are called:**

a) segmented prices.

b) reference prices.

c) relationship prices.

d) basing-point prices.

Answer: (b)

108) **With respect to setting pricing amounts, the belief that individual digits in a product's price have symbolic and visual qualities that should be considered in setting price is linked to:**

a) psychological pricing.

b) promotional pricing.

c) symbolic pricing.

d) psychographic pricing.

Answer: (a)

109) **When the seller places products at no charge with a carrier and the title and responsibility pass to the customer who pays the freight, it is which type of pricing strategy?**

a) FOB-origin pricing

b) uniform-delivered pricing

c) zone pricing

d) basing-point pricing

Answer: (a)

110) **_____ is a geographical pricing strategy in which the company charges the same price plus freight to all customers, regardless of their location.**

a) FOB-origin pricing

b) uniform-delivered pricing

c) zone pricing

d) basing-point pricing

Answer: (b)

Model Question Papers

M.B.A.

(Semester - II)

Marketing Management

Model Question Paper - 1

Time: 2¹ᐟ² Hours   Max. Marks:50

Instructions to the candidates:-

1) **All questions are compulsory.**
2) **Each question carries 10 marks.**

Q. 1. What is New Product Development? Explain the need for New Product development and reasons for failure of new product development.

OR

Q. 1. What is channel design decision? Discuss in detail the steps involved in channel design decisions.

Q. 2. Identify & briefly describe the four promotional methods an organization can use in its promotional mix.

OR

Q. 2. Channel intermediaries are essential for effective distribution of a product? Discuss. Explain in detail the role of marketing channels in marketing.

Q. 3. What do you mean by Marketing Evaluation and Control? Explain the marketing control procedure.

OR

Q. 3. What is Brand and branding? Elaborate the various branding decisions available to the marketers.

Q. 4. Write short Notes on following

    a) Geographical Pricing.

    b) Integrated Marketing Communication.

        OR

    a) Marketing Audit

    b) Logistics.

Q. 5. Explain in detail "The New Product Development Process".

OR

Q. 5. Explain the role of marketing communications in marketing effort.

Model Question Paper – 2

Time: 2¹ᐟ² Hours   **Max Marks: 50**

Instructions to the candidates:-

1) All questions are compulsory.
2) Each question carries 10 marks.

Q. 1. Define the term Product Life Cycle. And explain the strategies involved at various stages of Product Life cycle.

OR

Q. 1. Explain the term Pricing. Which internal and external factors influence the setting of the price of a product?

Q. 2. What are the various levels of marketing channels? Discuss the types of distribution strategies available to marketers for marketing channels selection.

OR

Q. 2. Define the term logistics. Enumerate its scope and objectives.

Q. 3. What is mean by marketing Audit? Explain the steps undertaken during an audit in detail.

OR

Q. 3. What is Integrated Marketing Communication? Explain the various elements of Integrated Marketing Communications.

Q. 4. Define Product. Explain different types of products with suitable examples.

OR

Q. 4. Highlight the role and importance of 'advertising' in promotional mix and explain various media of advertising used by a consumer durable company.

Q. 5. Discuss in detail the setting of pricing.

OR

Q. 5. Write a short note on followings

    a) Direct Marketing.

    b) Brand Elements

Model Question Paper - 3

Time: 2 ¹/²Hours   Max. Marks: 50

Instructions to the candidates:-

    1) All questions are compulsory.

    2) Each question carries 10 marks.

Q. 1. Explain the problems in Price setting. Pricing decision is a dynamic decision and not a Static one - Comment.

OR

Q. 1. Explain the term labeling with definition. And discuss its role in product management

Q. 2. What is Brand and branding? Elaborate the various branding decisions available to the marketers.

OR

Q. 2. Highlight the role and importance of 'advertising' in promotional mix and explain various media of advertising used by a consumer durable company.

Q. 3. Explain the role of marketing communications in marketing effort. How can an organization develop an effective communication process?

OR

Q. 3. Explain the objectives of preparing a Marketing plan. How does a marketer undertake product level planning?

Q. 4. Write short notes on following

    a) Promotional Pricing.

    b) Profitability Control.

OR

Q. 4. Explain price change. And discuss initiating and responding to price change from buyer's and competitor's point of view.

Q. 5. How can an organization develop an effective Communication Process?

OR

Q. 5. Explain in detail Franchise system. What are the benefits of franchising system?